SPIRIT MESSAGES
222 CHANNELED INSPIRATIONS

© 2017 by Shane Knox
All rights reserved

For author inquiries, contact
    Shane Knox
    Sage Studio 3.0
    5133 S. Campbell Avenue, Ste 203
    Springfield, MO 65810

www.mysagestudio.com

Text editing by Jann, Julius, and Hestia
Cover art, interior design, and layout by the Jesster

ISBN 978-1-944528-01-0

SPIRIT MESSAGES
222 CHANNELED INSPIRATIONS

by
Shane Knox, Shaman

Foreword by Jennifer Dove-Robinson

Foreword
by Jennifer Dove-Robinson

As human beings, finding our way home to the Self is the most important journey we ever take. And it's up to us to make that journey a conscious one. So, if you are holding this book in your hands, then it means that you are ready for a change in your life and that your journey has already begun.

Even though I am a multi-genre artist, a working writer, and an intuitive coach and counselor, years ago I hit a dead-end in my own personal development. I had heard of Shane Knox ("ShadowHawk," as he is known by his Shamanic name) and his work through a coaching colleague, and eventually he and I met on Skype. I was looking for someone with deep wisdom and compassion, because I knew there were intricate parts of both my physical body and my psyche that needed gathering and tending. I was in pieces on the floor of my own life and I knew I needed help.

The funny thing is that when Shane and I finally met, the first thing we said to each other was, "Hey, how have you been? It's been so long since I've seen you!" And then we both laughed, since we'd never met before. It was astounding to both of us to discover that we are kindred spirits, recognizing one another instantly, as if we'd already been working together for years.

Shane has clarity. His voice is deep and direct. Plus, he's funny. He makes his clients work. Period. And work, I did. I never questioned it. Together we dove in. And together we found me. We found the light and the darkness, we put the missing parts back together. He sent the hawk to take away the veil over my third eye so that I could finally see that I was, that I am, whole. Complete. Nothing about me needed to change for anyone else. And I could finally relax. Shane taught me that when we gather the lost or forgotten parts of ourselves together, we relieve others of the burden of having to do it for us. As a result of my work with Shane, I became a much better intuitive counselor and coach to my own clients.

Take all that is holy, all that is irreverent and profane, weld it to fire, add molten, unstoppable devotion, crown it with ink and leather, roll it all out on a Harley Davidson motorcycle, and that is Shane Knox. Shane is devoted to both self and other, to growth to the Divine. He trusts the information he receives and delivers it with both reverence and humor. His devotion also includes the pack of German Shepherds that he tends and the flock of birds that fill the air of his home. What a powerful symbol of his ability to live his life as a shaman, balanced always between the human and the animal, between the earth and the sky.

I'm familiar with soul retrieval. I'm familiar with psychics and intuitive healers. But it's refreshing to meet a man of deep integrity who walks his talk. It's not easy being a neo-shaman in today's world. It's not easy to carry one's beliefs and do one's work openly, where all can see. It makes us vulnerable.

Remember all those great talks you had with your Dad about your life and your decisions and exactly what to do next? Yeah, me neither. My dad was a wonderful man, but he mostly led by example and didn't usually sit me down for good long talks or advice. This book you are holding reads like it was written by the wisest of fathers. It's pointed, direct, generous, fierce, and compelling. On the surface, each of these 222 lightning strikes of insight holds a clear lesson. But upon further reading and meditation, more spacious layers of truth are revealed and you are invited to bring your own interpretation forward.

You can use this book as an oracle to support you each day for the rest of your life. It provides a scaffolding and support for change. Open it to any page and there is the encouragement you need, there is the answer to your question. The voice that rings through each of the channeled messages is loving, comforting, and grounding. We all need a friend, a mentor, an elder, to hold the mirror up to our own greatness, our own capacity for radiance.

This book supported me when I needed it the most. I was living through a time of deconstruction, when the foundation of my life as I had known it was dissolving. For over a month I consulted this beautiful book as my oracle, and I continue to open it daily. In it I find the exact words I need to begin to rebuild the ground of my own life and, like a garden, I am planting in new ground. As our country and the world around us experience this time of massive change, no matter what your beliefs might be about those changes, this book can help keep you grounded and sane.

I am deeply grateful for the light that shines through each of these messages channeled by ShadowHawk. As you embark on your own journey of personal growth and the quest to experience yourself as whole, I hope that you will find the deep abiding comfort that you so richly deserve.

Ways to Read This Book

Some books are meant to be devoured quickly and whole, while others are meant to be tasted and savored, one page at a time. In writing this book, I took dictation. Over 222 days, I was given Spirit Messages to write down. Each page marks a day's worth of mindfulness—for me in writing, and now for you in reading.

These Messages seek to reawaken your Soul knowledge to what you always already knew, though worldly cares and "noise" have often distracted you from that knowledge that is your birthright. But reading's not enough, if by "reading" you tend to think of a passive reception or consumption of "news." Spiritual insights have no meaning, unless they engage your own inward sight.

It's not what's on the page that matters, but what happens within you as you read and ponder and seek applications. Turn your reading into an experience that changes you as you experience it! The blank pages leave you room to add your own Spirit-guided insights. Write these down as they come to mind: make this a diary-record of your daily mindfulness. Invite your higher Self and Spirit Guides to read along with you—they'll be pleased and honored by the invitation. Ask questions of the text, and ask to be led to your own Soul's answers. With the book closed, shuffle through the pages like you were shuffling through a Tarot deck— the page that opens may hold your Soul's reply.

You'll note that some Messages repeat throughout. These are of special importance to us in our World today—and they are among the hardest for us to learn and put into practice. Remember, though, that your own Soul already knows everything contained in this book! This book is merely a reminder, offered in a series of Messages and Meditations.

LIVE FULLY IN THE MOMENT

Living fully in the moment: it's one of the greatest gifts we can give ourselves.

So often, our present joy gets stolen by past regrets or fears over the future.
By keeping our focus here and now, we free ourselves to greater joy.

Yes, we can learn from the past and we should prepare for the future.
But all lessons and plans are useless when our focus strays from the present.

Mistakes of the past serve no purpose if they do not change our present actions.
Likewise, we cannot hope to change our future experiences if we do not change the ways we act in the here-and-now.

So, take a deep breath and feel yourself fully present—here and now.

Become that breath: pay attention to your body sensations.
See, hear, smell, touch, taste the world around you.

Let go of past regrets and future cares.
And give yourself fully to the present moment.

This is freedom.

2
LET EXPERIENCES NOURISH THE SOUL

We place value in worldly success and in completion of worldly tasks when, in truth,
our Souls hunger for experience.

What you may perceive as failure on the physical plane
your Soul sees as opportunity for growth and greater understanding.
When we choose to validate our efforts, every step of the way,
we resonate with our Soul-Self.
We open ourselves to a new way of viewing life's challenges and
move a step closer to unity with our true nature.

Strive for greatness, do your best, always.

There is no failure except for the lack of trying.

Celebrate your victories and your mistakes, together.
Embrace both as part of your collective experience and rest comfortably
in the knowledge that your Soul has gained from the moment.

3

RECLAIM YOUR TRUE NATURE

We marvel at the beauty and majesty of nature.

The sound and spray of the waterfall, the scented breeze,
the glinting light of sunrise, the starlit night sky:
when we experience these,
we bear witness not just to the beauty and majesty
but to the mystery contained within nature.

How often we forget that we are an intrinsic part of nature—
of the very beauty we admire.

Our Souls incarnate into these bodies,
so that we can experience the beauty of Creation.

So, embrace yourself as a part of the incredible Creation we call life,
and live it as fully as you can.
Embrace every experience—even the bad ones—as a gift from your Soul.
Reclaim your identity as part of the mysterious oneness that encompasses all things.

This is your true nature.

REMAIN TRUE TO YOUR HIGHER BELIEFS

One of the best ways to be happy is to bring yourself into alignment
with what you believe.

So often we lose our true Self through peer pressure and
a desire to be liked or accepted.

Though it is difficult to remain true to our higher beliefs
in a world that constantly challenges them,
we have an inner sense of what is right, and what is not right, for our own selves.

When we speak or act in ways that don't match our inner knowing,
we distance ourselves from our Soul identity and fall into unhappiness.

But when we remain true to ourselves and
bring harmony to our thoughts, feelings, and actions,
we step into a state of joy that lies beyond society's acceptance or approval.

Give yourself permission right now to live in a way
that honors what you know is right for you.

And give this same permission to everyone you meet.

This is the path of joy.

5

VALUE — AND VALIDATE — YOUR OWN NEEDS

So many of us put out tremendous effort for someone else
but will not put that same effort into ourselves.

Why is this?
Because we want to be accepted and liked by others and
do not believe they will want us in their lives
unless we work to gain their favor.

Why then do we not do things for ourselves?

Because we do not fully like and accept ourselves.
We don't place the same value on our own needs as we do on the needs of others.
By putting the same time and effort into our own self, we develop a sense of
inner validation that leads to greater self-worth and self-love.
Once we begin to repair our relationship with our inner Self,
we open doors to new experiences in this life.

Decide today that the acceptance you want is within your own Self,
and that you, yourself, are worth the same efforts
you would put forth for another.

Do something beautiful for yourself today.
Do that thing you have put off because you don't feel you deserve it.
Be selfish for all the right reasons.

You will not only change your life,
but you will find yourself energized and recharged
and able to help others.

6
LISTEN TO YOUR INNER VOICE

Deep within each of you is a sense,
a knowing that recognizes truth.

It is the part of you that knows right from wrong
beyond the need for rules and society's morals.
It is the truest aspect of yourself that is connected ultimately to Spirit.

By developing the ability to hear and trust that inner knowing,
you will always be led along the path that feeds your Soul.
You will know integrity and be freed from difficulty in making decisions
as your inner compass guides you in all situations.

Take time in silence to learn to listen to your inner voice.

Do not let others dictate what is right for you.
This will often be based on their desires rather than on your best interest.
At a minimum, it will be based on their perspective instead of yours.

Do not give in to urges and temptations
that lead you away from what you know is right.

Learn to trust yourself,
even when others doubt you.

7
BE ONE WITH NATURE

We marvel at the beauty and majesty of nature
while forgetting that we are an intrinsic part of the very thing we admire.

Our Souls incarnate into these bodies
so that we can experience the wonders of Creation.

The sound of the waterfall, the breeze on our skin,
the beauty of sunrise, the starlit sky:
each holds its beauty because we experience it.

We bear witness to the majesty of nature:
such is our human task while on this plane.

Embrace yourself as part of this wondrous Creation
that we call life and live it as fully as you can.
Embrace every experience as a gift to your Soul,
both the good and the seeming bad.
Reclaim your identity as part of the great Oneness
that encompasses all things.

This is your true nature.

8

RISE ABOVE IT ALL

Some people will
go to great lengths to take you from your path.
Rise above it.

Some people will
question you and your character.
Rise above it.

Some people will
try to change you to fit what they want and,
when they can't, they will try to pull you down.
Rise above it.

Some people will try to drag you into their personal, petty dramas.
Rise above it.

By rising above it all, we step into our own power.
By staying true to ourselves and our higher natures,
we free ourselves from the karma and negative energies of others.
It is a challenge to remain true to ourselves,
especially when it means letting go of someone we once cared for.
But it is more than worth it.
When we choose not to give in to others' negativity,
we honor our true, higher Selves.

In staying true to ourselves,
we rise up to a state of grace and experience a greater connection
to the Soul-self—And that connection can help change
the very world we live in.

CLAIM YOUR PLACE

If you knew how beautiful and
full of potential you are in the eyes of your Spirit guides,
you would never doubt or limit yourself again.

You are limitless potential.

You are the light of the Universe.

You are a Soul expressing itself on this earth.

You are inherently beautiful—
a wondrous being capable of creating experiences beyond your imagination.

Claim your place in this world.

Claim your identity
as a bright shining light of the Spirit
and let yourself thrive.

Know in this very moment that all is as it should be
and that what happens next is far more in your control
than you have believed.

10
CELEBRATE YOUR UNIQUENESS

There is something unique within you,
something that wants to be set free.

Maybe it's a talent or an ability or
an idea you would like to express or create.
So often we allow fear and doubt to keep us from giving life to our true potential.
Sometimes we're afraid that we won't be appreciated or that we'll fail.

But some of the greatest accomplishments in human history came from Souls
that found boldness to stand apart from everyone else
and gave their truth a chance to thrive.

Decide today that you will no longer deprive the world
or yourself of the amazing things you are capable of.

Embrace your difference.

Use it to set your Soul free into a place of expression and joy.

Tell everyone you can about what makes you different
and celebrate that uniqueness
every chance you get.

11
SEEK WITHIN

Do not look for love.
That is an impossible quest.

Instead, be loving and the right person will find you.

Do not change for the sake of another's acceptance.
He or she may not give it, despite of your efforts.

Instead, accept yourself fully,
and those who appreciate your uniqueness
will gather around you.

Do not place happiness in things outside of yourself.
Your outer world constantly shifts and changes.
Instead find your happiness within
and free yourself from circumstances.

Seek what is within you,
what cannot be found in other people, places, or things.

Only when we look within shall we ever find what we seek.

In that moment the entire Universe will shift,
and what you have discovered within will be reflected back
to you—your inner and outer worlds
will become harmoniously one.

12
FLY FREE

Free is your natural state of being and yet,
far too often, you go to great lengths
to limit yourself through fear and doubt.
Many times this results in relationships
and situations that hold you
in a place that is not your truth.

Let go.

Face fear by finding your faith,
by remembering that you are a powerful being of light and potential
and step back into the freedom that is your birthright.

Choose no longer to put your energies into something that limits you:
Rather, invest yourself fully in living in freedom
and happiness.

Instead of giving energy to fear and anxiety,
focus on what uplifts you.

Fly free, beautiful Spirit.

This is your true state of being.

13
CELEBRATE YOUR BODY

Do not speak or think negatively
of your body.

It is an amazing vehicle
that your Soul has chosen to experience this lifetime.

So many of you live in anxiety and loathing
of your own most precious possession
through comparison to others.

Some even try to distance themselves
from their physical self in the name of spirituality.

What could be more spiritual than acceptance of the self?
What greater joy could there be than self-love?
Striving for betterment is a wondrous thing,
but only when it is motivated out of self-love.

You, body and all, are beautiful.

You are a magnificent Soul expressing itself through
an equally amazing physicality.

Celebrate all parts of yourself equally.

This is the way to great joy.

14
OWN YOUR TRUTH

How can you ever have trust in another if you lie to yourself?
Trust is something that must first be established within.

People lie to themselves out of fear, or a feeling of not being in control,
or a concern that others won't like them if they knew the truth.

Then people suffer from feeling that others are not honest with them, as well.
This inner seed of distrust extends to others far too often.

Decide today that, regardless of what the truth is in your life, you are going to own it.

Step into truth and become the truth you seek in others.
Trust in Spirit enough that you begin to own even the things in your world
that aren't quite as you want them to be.
Be honest with yourself and your life will become filled with a beauty
that far surpasses the image you created in falsehood.

Through this inner honesty,
you will begin to magnetize people, drawing them into your life.
And your ability to trust will grow.

15
VISIT YOUR TEMPLE

Within your heart space rests a magnificent temple—
the temple of love, from which the light of your Soul shines.

When you dwell within this space, you are at one with your true nature.
You step into the realization that you are not your possessions,
your occupation, or your challenges.

When the path you choose to walk in life emanates from this space,
you are walking hand in hand with Divinity.
Your expression becomes one of compassion and acceptance for yourself and others.
The struggles of life seem easier and joy begins to fill your World.

Go within.

Visit your temple often.
Let it uplift and recharge you.

Let that returning to your true self determine the pathway of your life
and step onto the road of great happiness.

16
ACCEPT YOUR LIFE

Do not waste your time wishing things were different in your life.
Every situation in your world is an opportunity to dig deeper into your personal truth,
a chance to learn more about your Soul's journey.

Some of the greatest gifts in this life come in ugly wrapping paper.
It is only when we open them fully,
revealing the core of what is inside,
that we are able to appreciate each circumstance
and lessons that come with it.

Do not avoid the uncomfortable and the difficult.
They will make you stronger.

Do not avoid that which is sad.
It will teach you the value of happiness.

Anger brings with it the chance to learn self-control.

Once you have accepted the circumstance
and learned what it has come into your life to teach you,
only then you will be free, through your intention
and actions, to change it.

17
REMEMBER YOUR TRUE PURPOSE

What is the meaning of life? What is my purpose?
These are two of the biggest questions people ask.

You are here to love, to laugh and cry,
to dance and sing, to mourn and celebrate.
You are here to share and be selfish, to struggle and suffer,
to find amazing joy and also great loss.
You are here to experience the wonders of nature,
the pleasures of treasured company,
and the tranquility of being alone with your thoughts.

You are here to be a friend, a lover, a family member.
Some will love you and some will hate.
You will feel sadness and regret.

Through all of this, you are to live life fully and give your Soul
opportunities to express its uniqueness on this Earth.
In so doing, you'll learn that your Soul is timeless and perfect,
interconnected to all things.

Through the joys and hardships of this life,
you will be turned back to this Soul-awareness.

You will remember that all you experience on this Earth
is a path leading you back to your true Self.

Remembering your true Self:
What greater purpose or meaning could there be?

18
WELCOME THE KIND WORDS OF OTHERS

Do not deflect compliments or praise.

Many do this out of a sense of humility when,
in fact, such humbleness is a reflection of insecurity:
people who cannot see their own incredible beauty
cling to their doubts and negative self-image.

In deflecting praise, you have not only denied yourself
a chance to feel validation and acceptance,
you have also denied others the joy of offering positive energy
in the form of compliments or kind actions.
This is a rejection of your own true nature and of theirs, as well.

You are a magnificent being.
You are a bright, shining Soul and,
regardless of how you may see yourself, you are praiseworthy.
Your life is cause for celebration.

Welcome the kind words of others and greet them with gratitude.
Keep the circle of positive energy moving and growing.
Find yourself in the compliments others offer you.

Let their words and gestures toward you be a reflection
of the truth you now see within your own self-image.

19

FIND COMPASSION FOR ALL

Compassion comes easily
when directed toward the less fortunate,
especially in regard to status or wealth.

Many find ease in generosity and
acceptance of those they see as beneath themselves.

Can you also find compassion for your equal
who has wronged you or who is simply different from you?
Can you find compassion for yourself for your differences from others
or for the goals you've not yet met?
Can you be compassionate in all areas of your life unconditionally?

Compassion isn't about acceptance.
You can wish that a person, a situation, or even your own self were different
and still find compassion in your heart for how things are.
Compassion is understanding: it is sharing in the awareness of basic human struggle.

Everyone meets challenges in life, and everyone tries their best.
Often, their best falls below your own standard.

Find compassion for all, in all.

Honor the effort, the personal struggle,
even of those who offend you.
This is an energy that, when given freely,
feeds your own Soul.

This is the path of Light.

20
FOCUS ON YOURSELF

Recognizing another's potential
in no way obligates them to live up to it.
Trying to change another to fit your definition of what is right
not only negates their personal expression;
it often becomes a means of self-distraction
from the things you wish to change within yourself.

Often, the frustration felt in leaving one's own potential unfulfilled
is projected onto others,
resulting in irritation, judgment, or anger.

Instead of trying to change the behavior of others,
choose to focus on yourself.

Take responsibility for your own happiness,
instead of basing it on the actions of others.
This will change your experience in this life.

In some circumstances,
happiness will come from acceptance of another's difference.
In others, it will come from no longer allowing them presence in your life.

When you shift focus to the Self, a great blessing occurs.
You move into an energy that feeds your Soul.

You become more accepting of differences in others
while discerning what is acceptable
in your World.

21
CREATE YOUR TRUTH

Your past is a roadmap of where you have been,
not where you are going.
You do not have to be defined by it.

So much time is wasted regretting past actions and events.
Take that time and energy and use it to create a new truth for yourself.
You are capable of far more than you believe.

You can choose to repeat past mistakes and patterns,
or you can decide here and now how you will be different.
Each day is a blank canvas to be filled in by your thoughts, words, and deeds.
Each day is a new opportunity to change your World, your expression.

You are empowered by Spirit with free will and creativity.
Do not squander such power by not living your new truth to the fullest.

You need no one's permission or approval.
You simply need clarity of intention,
and then follow through.

By embracing the present
and putting actions toward your new way of being,
you have already changed yourself.
By living in the now, freed from your past,
you have stepped onto the path of growth and change—
a path that will feed your Soul.

22

STAND STRONG

Standing in your truth with integrity
can be challenging at times,
especially when one is in touch with the Soul-Self
and seeking a Spirit-led life.

Others will try to drag you into their dramas,
their issues, and even their truths—
truths that do not match your own.
Some may try to change you to fit their desires.
Others will stoop to sabotage and insult.
In an effort to keep things as they were,
they may well question why you have changed.

Stand strong.
Do not be pulled into negativity.

Take that same energy and use it to strengthen your resolve
and live your truth even more fully.
Stand out from the crowd when integrity calls for it.
Take time to sit alone, quietly defining within yourself the life you want to live.
Find your truth of expression and establish that truth as your way of being.
Make it your response to the World.

Be prepared to shift your relationships.
Some will change. Some will end.

But through the strength of your resolve,
by the steadfast integrity of your truth,
you will begin to magnetize people into your life
and create situations that mirror
your higher vibration.

23
FOCUS ON THE SPIRITUAL

Everything in existence is Spiritual,
for everything in Creation is that which you call God.
It is in everything.
It is the sum total of everything that is or could be.

God is both the creator and the Creation,
the situation and the experience.
Within you, it is your Soul.

You are a part of this Divine tapestry,
and everything you place your focus on,
everything you experience, is Spiritual.

Everything in your World is there to remind you
that you are part of something much greater.
Once this belief is deeply established,
you will begin to see your World differently.
You will understand higher and lower vibrations,
freed from judgment.

What you send out comes back to you.

When you are at a high vibration, things go well; you feel in tune.
When you are in a lower vibration, you will be brought into anger or sadness,
maybe even a feeling of being lost or detached.

Both are deeply Spiritual states of being.
Both will ultimately lead you to your true Self
and to the understanding that you—
and everything that happens in your life—
is an act of Divine grace,
ever leading you back home.

24

CHOOSE YOUR COMPANY WISELY

Just as similar birds flock together and wolves run in packs,
so people thrive most when in the company of those like themselves.
By seeking out people who mirror your truths back to you and
inspire you to even greater heights, you choose to be blessed.
You empower yourself to grow and expand your experience in this life.
By establishing and relying on this network of support
and understanding, you define yourself
and find encouragement and validation
in times of need.

Far too often, people seek acceptance from people who just happen to be there
and change themselves to fit in, merely out of fear of being alone.
In such casual company, they will inevitably suffer from feelings
that they are misunderstood or lacking in approval.

Choose your company wisely!

Anyone holding a significant place in your life
should be uplifting and supportive.
This does not mean you have to match in every way.
Even right-minded criticism can be a blessing
when it is coupled with understanding and acceptance.

Make the choice now to surround yourself
and interact with those who complement your own energy,
who recognize and honor your truth.

Know yourself well enough to know who fits in your circle of support
and treasure those individuals.
Hold love and compassion for all you meet,
but be selective in whom you invite along on this grand journey
you call life.

25
STEP INTO THE DANCE

In the quest for Spirituality,
many judge themselves for becoming caught up
in the human experience,
for giving in to emotion, reaction, or ego.
If they do not live up to their higher values and beliefs,
they feel a sense of failure.
They may even attempt to separate their higher values
from their daily lives.
This is a hurtful perspective.

When you choose to see everything in your World—
the preferable and the uncomfortable,
the "success" and the "failure,"
ALL—
as aspects of your Soul's journey,
you step into Divine Grace.

You begin to see everything in your World
as a grand master teacher,
a constant presence of guidance
and reassurance leading you back to yourself.

You begin to realize that everything in existence
is part of a great oneness
and that you are as important as any other aspect of Creation.

Your experience—all of it—is a divine dance.
It is the journey of a Soul as experienced from the human perspective.

Be grateful for every part of your life.
It is all there for a reason.
The fact that you exist is proof of the magnificence of Spirit.

26

FORGIVE FOR YOUR OWN SAKE

Forgiveness is a very powerful energy
that is capable of changing your life.

Finding the compassion to acknowledge that the other person's wrongdoing
reflects his or her own inner struggle
releases you from the cycle of negativity.

This does not mean accepting the behavior
or even allowing the person's presence in your life.
It does mean finding your own inner challenges—
the things you wish to overcome and have not,
the things for which you must forgive yourself—
in order to extend that understanding to others and to find peace.

For your own sake, offer forgiveness.

Forgiving others frees you from negative energies
connected with the situation
and fills you with a compassion
that will allow you to view your own struggles
more kindly.

27

OWN YOUR MISTAKES

Owning mistakes and taking responsibility for your actions—
especially when they are wrong—
is an act of empowerment.

So many avoid owning their errors out of vanity
and a need to control their image in the eyes of others.
They are simply afraid of looking bad.
In doing so, they step out of truth.

Your mistakes are opportunities to learn
and redefine yourself.
They give you a chance to understand yourself
and the effect you have on others.

By acknowledging error and apologizing,
you will have stepped into a space of true self-ownership,
a state of a Divine Grace.
You will have let go of the fear
of how you are seen
and increased your personal awareness.

Do your best, always.

Let that be your goal instead of
worrying about image,
and remember that the very nature of
Spirit is forgiveness
and understanding.

28

LIVE FULLY IN THE MOMENT

One of the greatest gifts we can give ourselves
is to live fully in the moment.

So often our present joy is stolen
by past regrets or fears over the future.

By choosing to focus on the here and now,
we free ourselves into a greater experience.

Yes, we can learn from the past and we should prepare for the future,
but these are useless if we lose focus on the present.

Past mistakes serve no purpose if they do not change our present actions.
We cannot hope to change our future experiences if we do not act differently now.

Take a deep breath and let go of everything but the now.
Be fully present in this very moment.
Experience your world fully.

This is freedom.

29
KNOW YOU ARE NOT ALONE

When you feel alone in your struggles,
it is because you have forgotten
that you are connected to all that is.

You do not have to face your challenges by yourself.
Spiritual help is always available if you will seek inwardly.
We are always with you and eagerly wait for such opportunities
to offer you love, guidance, and support.

When you acknowledge your connection to Spirit
the answers you seek will be everywhere.

You will begin to hear us speaking to you
through every voice, song, and written word.
The Universe will conspire to hold you up on your path
and lead you to your truth.
Your answers will be clear
and the right actions made evident.
People and events will align.

Know that this is truth
and that you are blessed and loved.

Know that you are not alone.

30
DON'T GIVE UP

Perseverance is one of the most powerful energies
in the Universe.

So many simply give up or fail even to try,
if things are not easy or they find obstacles to their desires.
Often, people will let go of their dreams because they find the path challenging.

Some of the most amazing accomplishments in human history have come from people
who failed in their first attempts but found the courage to try again or to try differently.

Decide that your goals are worth effort, perseverance, and diligence.
Validate your own efforts and be willing to regroup and try again.
Surround yourself with support and encouragement.

Don't give up.

The World needs your contribution,
no matter how private
or personal it may seem.

31
SEE THE WORLD AS YOUR MIRROR

Your outer World is a reflection
of your inner Self.

If you wish more fully to understand yourself,
begin by understanding the people and situations in your life.
They are all there because you need the experience they offer
to further you in your Soul's journey.
This is especially true of the people and situations
you find troublesome or annoying.

Make peace with that part of yourself,
and your experience with others will change.

When you begin to see the things in your life as a grand design
rather than as random occurrences,
you will have stepped onto the path
of self-awareness and mastery.

Find the beauty inside of you
and watch it radiate out into the World.

It can be no other way.

32

LET GO OF THE OLD TO EMBRACE THE NEW

Only by letting go of what is
will you be able to grasp what could be.

Many cling to the familiar
even when it is uncomfortable
or when they know
that it is no longer their truth.

Fear and uncertainty will hold them in a place of stagnation
and will keep them from knowing true happiness,
even when change is what they claim to want.

For others, the lack of external support and validation
will keep them from making real changes.
For some, it comes down to simple laziness and lack of ambition.

Your potential means nothing if it is not acted on.

Let go of the old to embrace the new.
In that moment, you will understand
empowerment, freedom, and joy.

33

BLESS OTHERS

Never discount your ability
to make a difference in someone else's life.
Often a smile, a kind word, or a bit of encouragement
is all one needs to be uplifted
and set on a grander path.

Be the very thing you seek.

If you want kindness in your World,
show compassion to others.
If you need validation,
offer your support to someone else.
If you want love, be loving.

Giving your time and offering your attention
are the highest forms of tithing.
Remember that everything and everyone is connected.

By blessing others you have already blessed yourself.
By giving freely, you have not only helped someone else,
you have opened yourself
to receive freely as well.

311

KNOW YOURSELF

To say that you will deal with something later
is to deny yourself happiness in the here and now,
for your truth will not wait.
It will whisper to you from every corner of your life.
It will call to you.
It will become the thing you cannot ignore.

Know, then, that you are a traveler on the road to the Self
and that you are the road being traveled.
You are the roadblocks along the way
and you are the solution to those blocks.
You are the starting point and the destination.

You are the experience and that which is being experienced.
You are the situation and every emotion connected to it.
You are the only one who can understand your perspective,
your experience, and your reasons for your actions.

You are the breath in the moment that is the essence of physical life.
You are a Soul expressing itself in human form.

You came into this life with a Divine purpose,
and you chose every circumstance that you encounter.
Why then do you allow yourself to feel
that you are not in control of yourself,
of your World?

35

DECIDE NOW

Every time you are confronted with a challenge,
you have choices.

Will you give into old habits and patterns,
or will you embrace personal change?
Is this the moment that you follow your highest inner knowing
of what is right for you?
Or will you give in to lower energies of fear,
doubt, and insecurity?
Is now the time you decide to win
the battle with yourself?

Decide now on the person you choose to be.

Allow yourself to break free of outmoded mindsets
and limiting beliefs about what you are capable of.
Establish your chosen identity and allow strength of conviction to
empower you for real and lasting change.

When you do this,
you will see life-situations as opportunities
rather than challenges.

36

CREATE YOUR WORLD

When you find yourself in a situation
other than what you desire,
remember the journey that brought you there.

The Universe is not punishing you,
nor will it reward you.
It is simply reflecting back to you your choices,
expectations, and actions.

By placing the blame
for what you encounter outside of yourself,
you are letting go
of the ability to change it.

What you experience is a result of the vibrations
you are sending out into the World.
What you experience is the reflection
of your own inner Self.

Only when you stop punishing yourself
will the World stop punishing, as well.

By letting go of the belief
that things can be no other way,
you will have freed yourself
to create a World more of your own choosing.

37

DECIDE THAT YOU MATTER

The moment you decide that you matter,
that you are worthy of happiness,
is the moment your life will change forever.

In that moment of self-validation,
everything shifts.
You will begin
to find guidance everywhere
that leads you back to your truth.
You will find strength of Spirit
that will support you in that truth,
and opportunity
will open everywhere for you.

Your life will become a rich adventure
with a deep understanding
that the Soul is being fed
by your very existence.

Circumstance and situation
will no longer dictate your experience,
and you will begin to see every moment as an opportunity
to explore and to validate yourself again and again
in a cycle of constant growth
and eventual enlightenment.

38
BE WHAT YOU WANT TO EXPERIENCE

People will disappoint you.

They will act selfishly.
They will say one thing and do another.
You will sometimes be left
with burdens caused by others.
Life will seem unfair.

In these moments,
you have a choice.
You can allow the situation to change you,
or you can choose to change the situation.

No matter what is happening in your life,
decide to give better than you get.
Establish an energy of integrity
and be an example to the World.

Set your mind on being what you want to experience
and what you want to receive.
Act in that way, and what you want will become your life.

By taking responsibility to act according to your integrity
instead of reacting to situations,
you will have begun to master the Self on a very deep level.
You will have freed yourself from the actions of others
and empowered yourself
to find true happiness.

39
LET GO OF GUILT AND WORRY

Guilt and worry are both thieves
that rob you of your ability to live in the moment.
Guilt holds you in your past,
while worry obsesses about the future.
Neither allows focus on the only point in time
when change can occur—the present.
What is most troublesome
is that both past and future
are constructs of your own mind.

The guilt you carry is self-imposed.
You can free yourself from it through sincere apology
or not repeating past mistakes.
Often you'll find it is a burden you are carrying alone,
with no one else holding you to blame,
or with the offended party having already forgiven you.

Likewise, much of what you worry about
will never come to pass.
It, too, exists only in your mind.

By unbinding yourself from these energies,
you are free to focus on the now.
When you do so, you are able to create your World
in a way where you have learned from your past
and are proactive in creating a future without feelings of negativity.

Let go of guilt and worry and step fully into your present Self.
Create your World from that perspective, and you will live a much happier life.

40

LIVE IN FAITH

Establish faith in the Divine,
in God, and in Spirit;
decide within yourself what these mean to you.
Leave room for exploration and growth
within your beliefs.

Form a relationship with the Divine,
starting with some practice of dedication.
Have a conversation with God.
Pray, meditate, chant, serve, tithe—do something for God!
Make faith an active energy in your life.
Make it part of your expression.
Extend it to others.

Find Spirit within yourself
and radiate its light into the World.
There will be times when faith will be all you have.

When you practice faith as a way of life,
it will become so much a part of you
that it will hold you up in difficult times.
You can count on it to help you persevere,
to thrive, to change.

When you live in faith,
that very faith will help you live.

41
TAKE TIME TO PLAY

Remember to take time
in your busy life for enjoyment.

Relax, embrace silliness, play!

In your quest for goals and success,
you often forget about the joys that life offers.
Problems and worries steal your ability
to let loose and simply have fun.

Don't take yourself so seriously.
Yes, you should have goals,
work through problems,
and deal with the hardships of life.
These things are essential.

But you must balance them with times of pure enjoyment.
This is especially true when you have made accomplishments in your life:
do not rush to the next task on the list.
Allow yourself a celebration, however brief.

Decide that you are going to make
happiness and joy your priorities in life,
and follow that up with action!

Do something fun and allow it to feed your Soul.
When you live in this way,
you will create an energy of joy
that will affect what comes
into your life.

42
REMEMBER COMPASSION

Everybody hurts in a unique way.
Remembering this will help you to find compassion
for others and for yourself.

When faced with struggles and challenges,
we often do not show our best to the World.
Our pain and struggles often affect
our interactions with others.

This is true in reverse, as well.
It is impossible to know
what another person is going through, inside.

Acknowledging your own shortcomings with others
and finding the root cause of a particular action of yours
will not only free you from repeating that same action,
but it will also help you to understand the hurtful actions of others.

This does not necessarily mean acceptance.
You have a right to decide what energies
and people you allow into your life.

Forgive yourself for actions motivated out of suffering
and extend that to everyone you meet.
This is compassion.
This is love.

This is the true nature of Spirit.

43
CREATE YOUR INTENTIONS

Your intentions
have the power
to go far beyond your imaginings.

Your intentions create opportunities in your World.
Through actions and follow-through
you are able to actualize those opportunities
to create new experiences in your life.

Your Soul knows you are capable of far more
than you will allow yourself to realize.
Therefore, the opportunities you create
and the results of your intentions are far bigger
and can take you farther
than you have ever allowed yourself to dream.

Allow your higher Self to inspire your intentions.
Trust in the urgings of your Spirit.

Allow that awareness to be coupled with action,
and you will be led to a life
filled with wonder.

44

HONOR YOUR ONENESS WITH SPIRIT

What you refer to as the Creator
and the Creation are in fact one.

They are inseparable.

The great truth is that all things are one in Spirit.
You are connected to everything in existence
and, therefore, to the Source of All Creation.
This is a blessing and a responsibility.

If you devalue yourself in any way,
you are in fact devaluing all that is.
When you focus on faults within yourself,
you are implying that Spirit itself is flawed.
This cannot be true.

Self-criticism makes you feel separate from Spirit.
When you focus on flaws within yourself or in your outer World,
you lose awareness of being part of the All, part of perfection.

Begin by seeing yourself as a Divine being.
Honor that part of you that is connected to the All
and realize that everyone, everything that you experience
is also a part of that great connectedness.
Then, apply that reverence to your thoughts and actions.
Live from Spirit and take responsibility for the intentions, words,
and actions that you put into the creative force.
Know that you matter as much as anyone or anything else in all of Creation.

45

KNOW YOU ARE WATCHED OVER

Know that your loved ones
in Spirit
watch over you.
Know that they see and hear you,
that they do indeed walk beside you.

They share in your celebrations
and give love in times of mourning.
Always, they offer their support and guidance.

Watch for them to manifest
and speak through every available source.
Trust your intuition when you know they are near.
Watch for their messages to point you along your way.
Understand that, while you worry for their well-being,
they are watching over yours.

Soul is eternal.
It is the essence of who you are
and of all who remain.
All are threads
woven into the beautiful tapestry
of Spirit.

Within this tapestry,
celebrate your thread.
Know that your Soul-identity
will continue on.
Know that those whom you love
continue on beside you.

46

BE SLOW TO JUDGE AND QUICK TO VALIDATE

Do not live your life in fear of disappointing others
or in seeking validation from others.

Strive to do your best in all situations
and realize that you will disappoint some people sometimes,
no matter how hard you try.
This does not mean you have failed.

Likewise, others will disappoint you,
even when they have given their best.
Let the times when you have given great effort and fallen short
be a reminder when others
are in the same situation.

Begin to make choices
based on what you feel is right for yourself.
Decide that others are responsible
for their own happiness.

Be slow to judge and quick to validate,
both yourself and others.

This is the way of happiness.

47
THERE'S NO NEED TO EXPLAIN

You are responsible
for your thoughts, words, and actions.
However, you do not owe anyone else explanation
for your way of being.

Many people over-explain themselves
out of a fear of not being accepted.
Some feel the need for others to understand their struggles,
hoping it will change how they are seen.
Some offer excuses to deflect reality.

Whatever the reason, self-explanation
is a choice, not a mandate.
Do not allow others to make such a demand on you.
Nor should you demand explanation from others.

Your free will and personal experiences
have led to your expression and choices.
Only you can understand how these affect you
and motivate you as they do.

Take personal responsibility for your actions.
Share your experience with others when you want to.
Allow others to think what they will.

This will grant you freedom
you have not known before.

48

BE YOURSELF

Do not focus on what you don't like about yourself;
realize that you are far more than a list of shortcomings.
There is something about you right now
that others see as amazing.
Begin to see yourself in that same way.

You are magnificently flawed,
radiantly beautiful,
and clumsy in your own perfection.
Love your uniqueness.

Do not hide away out of shame or embarrassment.
Share your talents,
however humble you may think they are.
Everyone has a gift to share with the World.
It is one's own Self.

The World is better for having you in it.
Never allow yourself to feel you are less than others:
you are not lacking.

You, your life, your potential
are all miracles.
Celebrate your truth.
Honor your expression.
Be yourself.

This itself is its own reward.

49

MAKE LOVE A WAY OF LIFE

So many of you seek for love.
You look for another person
to give you the feelings of acceptance
and grace that love grants.
The truth is that love lies within you.
It is the essence of Spirit itself
and it resides within your heart space.

Embrace yourself as you are right now.
Open your heart unto your own Self
and know that, by your Divine heritage, you deserve to be loved.
Let go of everything that offends this truth.
When you find love for the Self, it grows until you cannot contain it:
you will begin to extend it to everyone you meet
in the form of service and compassion.

Loving becomes a way of life for the blessed.
When you live in this truth,
it is inevitable that the Universe will reflect this back to you
in the form of treasured friends, of family
that goes far beyond blood,
and often a lover that connects with you heart-to-heart.

Begin with yourself.
Love deeply.
Beyond that, love those in your life right now.
Make loving your way of life
and you will indeed grow to love your life.

The key to finding what you seek is to be that which you seek.

50
KEEP YOUR COMPOSURE

Anger is a perfectly acceptable emotion.
It is a degree of discernment
that helps you to define your own boundaries.
Indeed, some things should make you mad.
However, the loss of temper that is often called anger
is a loss of self-control.

People will offend you.
Situations will push you to response.
In these moments, be cautious to remain in control of yourself.
When you allow a circumstance to provoke you to anger,
you have given control of the Self over to the situation.

Retain mastery of the self.
Speak your truth clearly and without dramatics.
Establish your boundaries
and allow your anger to guide you instead of ruling you.
Allow yourself a fully human moment when you are angered,
but then respond by rising into a Spiritual response.
Remain true to yourself and to your higher way of being,
regardless of what you are confronted with,
regardless of what you feel.

51
SHOW AND TELL YOUR LOVE

Take the time today to tell someone that you love them.
So many people suffer from feeling unloved or unwanted.
Others may be having a difficult time that you are unaware of:
reaching out to them could make all the difference.

You are a being of love and light.
By expressing your love to those that you hold dear,
you are connecting with your Soul's truth.
There is much darkness in the World,
and this truth is the only thing that can change that.

Open your heart, even if you have been hurt.
Give love freely.
Say it out aloud.
Show it every way you can.

Make loving your way of being and love will flow back to you.
When love again becomes an easy and natural expression,
then the World you often envision and hope for will indeed become reality.
Decide today that your purpose beyond all other things
is to be a beacon and example of love.
Show everyone you meet a better way of living
through being a loving person.
Affect change in this way.

Love is the most powerful tool for change you have within you.
Share it with the World
and expect great things from it.

52

FIND YOUR TRUE FAMILY

Family often goes far beyond bloodlines.
Often one's relations with certain relatives
may become strained or even dysfunctional.
Even when related, people are individuals on their own paths.
Sometimes these paths move gracefully side by side or even overlap.
Others simply lead to different places.

Do not allow yourself to carry blame
when another person is unwilling to find common ground.
Be on good terms when you are able, but do not waste your time
trying to build closeness with the unwilling.
Instead, seek out your family of choice,
whether they are blood relatives or special friends.
Find those individuals who celebrate your uniqueness.
Seek the people who mirror your truth back to you with love and support.
Your true family recognizes each other on a Soul level.

Build your circle carefully and be certain
that those to whom you give your time,
attention, and love give as freely as they take.

Find the people you know you can count on.
This is true family.

53
ACT, DON'T REACT

Do not allow others to dictate your responses.
They are acting from their own inner desires,
which may or may not reflect your truth.
Your actions should come from your highest motivations,
rather than reaction to what another person says or does.
Do not so easily give your power away.

Likewise, respect others
by not trying to control their responses to the World.
In your quiet times of reflection, choose the person that you want to be.
Define yourself according to your highest thinking
and make that your way of being,
even when confronted with people or circumstances
that encourage you to act differently.

Let go of reaction and step into chosen action instead.
When you react, you are giving away your free will
and allowing situations and other people to define you.
Rather, allow your truth to become so strong
that you begin to change your experience
instead of its changing you.

54
ACCEPT YOURSELF

Real and lasting change
can only occur in your life when you fully love
and accept yourself as you are, here and now.
That does not mean you have to like your present circumstance;
but you do need to own yourself and the situation fully.
How could you hope to change something
you do not have real connection to?

When you accept yourself and your circumstance,
you are able to be in control of it.
When your desire for change is coupled with love of the Self,
then motivation becomes pure and change much easier.

Decide today that the only changes you seek
will be based out of love for yourself
instead of motivated by comparison to others
or society's expectations.
Changes that are based out of fear never last.
Moreover, they will never satisfy you in the reasons you wanted change.
They will only feed your response to fear itself.

Make loving and accepting yourself your way of life.
Let the changes you seek be motivated from this awareness.
In this way, you have already had great victory
before the changes you seek have begun.

55
SPEAK YOUR FEELINGS

Learn to communicate your feelings
and needs to those in your life.
Many people become frustrated or unhappy
because the people they care about seem to not respond to their needs.
This is often a result of the other person's simply not knowing
what is wanted.
Friendships, family, and lovers
have fallen victim to disappointment, simply because one party
feels injured without ever having communicated
his or her needs.

Do not assume that people know what is in your mind.
How could they?

Be open and honest.
Speak your feelings and needs clearly.

This type of sharing opens the door for deeper connection.
There will be times when people do not respond,
even if you have been quite clear.
In such moments you will learn a great deal about the other person
and can rest comfortably in the knowledge
that you upheld your side of the relationship
with honesty and directness.

56
GIVE UP REGRET

Do not spend your time focused on regret.
Of course, you should learn from your mistakes
and grow from your experiences.
Poor choices should not be repeated.

However, to obsess over feelings of guilt or regret
only feeds the cycle of negative energy.
It begins to tear down your self-image and can,
at times, make you feel like a bad person
instead of someone who has simply made a mistake.

Make amends with those you have wronged.
Forgive yourself and find gratitude for the opportunity
to shift your way of relating to others and to your Self.

Each day is a chance to rewrite your story.
Let this fresh perspective become your way of life.
Allow the past to guide you to a better future, but do so without regret.
Take the time and energy you would expend toward guilt
and use these to create something amazing.

In this way, you are able to take every wrong choice
or action and use it to make a better life.

57
LEARN TO LET GO

Stepping away from a person or situation in your life
may be difficult, even when you know it is the right thing.
So many times we create conflict or drama
because it's easier to let go in anger than in any other way.

We may be on the receiving end of this as well.
Quite often, the person or situation has disappointed
or hurt us in some way.

Don't think of disappointment or hurt
as reasons for walking away.
Instead, know that you are honoring the Self
and extending that same honor to the person or situation
that you are leaving.

In doing, so you charge the situation
with energies of growth, discernment, and respect.
These are incredible energies to use in building the next step of your life.

Remember: if it's not right for you,
let it go.
You'll be changing the situation
instead of letting it change you.

58
MEET CRITICISM WITH HONESTY

At times, you may fall victim
to other people's criticism or judgment.
This is an opportunity for awareness and perspective.
Realize that many people attempt to pull others down
instead of lifting themselves up.
They may do this
out of insecurity, envy, or a desire to hold you in an old identity
that serves their purposes.
In these instances,
their opinions have nothing to do with you.

At other times, the criticisms and judgments will be accurate
and a chance for you to learn more about Self.
The key to understanding the difference
is to establish within yourself absolute honesty.
When you choose to see yourself as you are
instead of how you wish you were,
you will gain honest perspective and personal truth.
This is no small undertaking.
It is, however, the key to lasting happiness.

Work diligently on finding the truth of your being.
Seek to understand your inner motivations.
Observe Spirit's reflection of your identity
and accept personal truth,
even when you desire change.
This will free you from the effects of harsh opinions
and empower you to create true,
uplifting changes in your life.

59
CREATE YOUR INNER PEACE

Peace of mind is
one of the greatest treasures you can have.
It is a state of being that grants calmness, clarity, and happiness.
However, you cannot seek out peace of mind.
Instead, you must create it by removing from your life
everything that is not peaceful.
Worry and fear, comparisons, and anger
are just a few of the energies that keep you from inner peace.

Begin to examine your life and interactions with others.
Let go of conflict and the need to be right.
Make amends whenever possible.

Live your truth comfortably and give up on dramatics.
Let go of people and circumstances
that pull you toward such things.
Root out of your life everything
that takes you away from the awareness
that you are a child of the Divine
and that you deserve peace.

In this way of being,
your life becomes like a beautiful, tranquil lake.
Things may disturb the surface,
but the calm underneath will smooth the ripples
and return the waters to peace and beauty.

60
CHOOSE OPTIMISM

Stop wearing your burdens like a badge of honor.
Choose not to define yourself by your problems and limitations.
Why give focus and energy to these things?
Why identify yourself by the worst parts of your life?
Complaint without action to remedy the circumstance is wasted energy—
it reflects a need for attention.

Your circumstances are what they are.
Your response to them determines what happens next.
Turn your effort to solutions instead of problems.
Speak of what is good in your life as often as you can.

Adopt an attitude of optimism.
Spend so much time in gratitude
that it takes on new meaning for you.
Look for the good in the World.

Your life is part of the beauty that exists so abundantly
when joy becomes your mindset.
Invest your focus, thoughts,
and efforts toward that awareness of joy.
Choose to be blessed and speak of yourself
as though you are.
Your reality will be quick to follow.

61
CONNECT WITH SPIRIT

Many people feel lost and lonely in life.
They may feel disconnected and sad
because they have forgotten their Divine heritage,
their connection to the All.
This need not be so.

By taking quiet time each day,
an inner path to happiness may be discovered.
This path leads to the true Self
and to the realization that you are a part of something
much larger than your experience.
Hold on to this awareness.

Accept that you are part of Spirit
and this inner path will lead to outer changes in your World.
Messages from Spirit will be everywhere you turn,
leading you to greater things.

Every song will sing answers to you.
Every conversation will reveal truths,
and your life will be filled with a sense of connection and wonder.
New people will be drawn into your life
and each will have a gift for you,
a reflection of your newfound truth.
By going within, you will discover Spirit
in every part of your World.
It has always been this way.
You need only remember.

62

OWN THE SELF

So many people blame others for their lack of joy.
They will speak of how they have been wronged
or how others force them to act in certain ways.
To live this way is to live in misery.

Know that you yourself
are responsible for your own happiness and well-being.

You are in control
of your choices, emotions, and actions, not someone else.
By allowing others to dictate your response,
you give away your power to change yourself
and your experience.

People will disappoint you.
Do not also disappoint yourself.
Even in the gravest of circumstances,
the Soul is capable of peace and joy.
Establish a deep connection to this part of your Self.
Embrace responsibility for your life.
Choose to be happy.

Give yourself permission to move on
instead of lingering in hurt
and troubled thoughts.
There is a great joy that comes
in the ownership of the Self.

63
SPEAK YOUR TRUTH

The truth need be accompanied by no apology,
no qualifier, or disclaimer.
It stands as an absolute.
Embrace this and find freedom in life.
Begin within.
Establish pure honesty with yourself.
Decide to let go of the inner lies, deceptions, and excuses.
Accept yourself fully and be completely real within your
perception of who you are.
Once you have found this degree of self-honesty,
extend it out into your World.

Calmly and kindly speak your truth
in every situation.
While always keeping compassion as your guide,
do not shrink from honest communications.
If you value those in your life,
honor them by being open
and direct with them.

Surround yourself with people
who share the value of honesty.
Choose in this moment to not feel injured by the truth.
Instead, let it inform and empower you.
Welcome the kind and constructive criticisms
that find their way to your awareness.
Build your life upon truth and you will always walk in integrity
and be blessed by Spirit.

64

LET YOUR LIGHT SHINE

In dark times of sorrow and despair,
it is often difficult to remember
that the light you seek resides within you.
It is your Soul's true nature to shine with the light of Spirit.
Life will at times be filled with challenges and heartaches.
It will also be filled with times of great joy.
In moments of happiness your light shines easily.
You will glow with satisfaction and feel that faith comes naturally.
You will believe that all is as it should be.

Remember these feelings when you face challenges.
Recall times when you felt your inner light.
Establish a regular practice of faith
and use it to help refocus your energies:
during times of difficulty,
think back to the goodness in your World.

Your Soul chose this life and these experiences.
Do not begrudge it of these.
Embrace your life fully, all of it.
Experience, learn, and grow.
This is why you are here.

Above all, let your light shine.
Choose to become a beacon of faith and hope
through the difficulties you face.
By embracing your inner light,
you can eliminate darkness from your life
and inspire others.
Both are great blessings.

65

LIVE SPIRITUALLY

Spirituality is not a passive state of being.
Living spiritually requires decisions and follow-through.
It requires that you set boundaries for yourself
and in regard to others.
Spirituality demands compassion and love.
It yearns for faith, humility, and selflessness.
It also thrives on self-fulfillment and self-expression.
These cannot exist simply as thoughts and ideals.
They must be put into action.

Yes, the spiritual path asks that you
find quiet times of meditation and inner reflection,
but it also asks for action.
You came here to live!
Make decisions and then follow through on them.
Communicate and enforce your boundaries
and honor those of others as a sign of respect to all you meet.
Show compassion in your interactions with others,
even those you do not agree with.

Make loving your way of being.
Make it an action instead of just an emotion.
Practice faith so strongly that others ask you about it.
Likewise, seek to express your truth.

By actively living your spirituality
instead of just holding concepts in your mind,
you will open your life to beauty
greater than you have ever imagined.

66
BE OPEN TO CHANGE

Your life is a series of never-ending changes.
Change is part of your very nature.
The fact that you are a Soul,
once formless but now residing within a physical body,
illustrates this truth.

Why then do so many resist change?
Often it is due to fear of the unknown
and a need to assert or maintain the illusion of control.
An amazing freedom comes when you choose
to embrace the changes that present themselves in your life.
Gracefully flowing from experience to experience
is the mark of one who trusts Spirit,
knowing that all is as it should be.

Even more blessed are those
who seek out change for personal betterment and growth.
Remember that people and situations
will come into your life and then leave
once the lessons are learned.

You are passing through this lifetime
on a journey that reaches into eternity.
Do not cling to the past or begrudge transitions.
These will come, regardless.
Open yourself fully to them.
Realize you are a child of Creation.
What you experience ultimately comes from
the core of your Being.
Welcome what you create next in your life
with grace and acceptance.

67

BE QUICK TO FORGIVE

To forgive is to free yourself from negativity.
It is a powerful tool
that can change your response to
and the effects of other people's actions.
When you cannot offer forgiveness,
you remain trapped in a cycle of negativity
and will continue to be affected by the person who hurt you.

When you forgive,
you take back control of your thoughts and emotions.
Forgiveness is not about acceptance or approval.
When wronged,
you are given the choice of how
to continue your interactions with the other person.
You may choose to establish and enforce boundaries,
or you may find it best to
limit or end the connection altogether.

Forgiving is ultimately an act of the Self, by the Self, for the Self.
To extend forgiveness to another is the mark of an awakened Soul but, ultimately,
those who hurt others must forgive themselves
before any change can occur in their lives.
They must connect with and understand
the wrong that they did.
In this same way, you must seek to forgive yourself
of your own wrongdoings.

Be quick to forgive.
Use forgiveness as an instrument of self-liberation.
Free yourself from the negativity of others in this way and your Soul will shine.

68
CREATE THE LIFE YOU CHOOSE

Every day that you draw a breath
is a chance to create yourself.
It is a chance to let go of what you have been
and embrace what you are capable of becoming.
You are a physical embodiment of the creative force,
a Soul within a human body.

Know that you are not separate from Spirit.
In fact you, and all that exists,
move in a great harmony of Creation.
When you begin to see the World in this way,
you open yourself to choose your expression
within Divine reality.

Know that your identity is of your own choosing,
free from definition outside of your own deepest vision of Self.
What others think of you does not matter.
Comparisons to others mean nothing.
Your past doesn't matter, either.
All that matters are your choices and your actions.

You are free to create the life you choose.
Everything that stands in your way
is no more than illusion.

69
LIFE IS NOT A COMPETITION

The only person
you are actually competing with is yourself.
The material possessions, achievements, and opinions of others
are nothing by which to judge your life.
Many people miss out on the joy
of finding their own voice and personal expression
because they base their happiness
on a comparison with others.
They may feel that someone else has more than they do
or that they have reason to envy another's experience.
They will try to look, talk, act, and quest for things
based on what they see in that other person's life,
desperately trying to do better and have more.
They will base their sense of achievement
on somehow winning this illusory contest.
This will not lead to success.
It can only lead to sadness.

Find your truth.
Find what makes you happy
and turn your focus to those things.
Let go of comparison and competition.
Strive only to best yourself.

Realize that the only real winner
is the person who decides not to enter the competition.
By giving up competition and comparison,
you will have reached a space
where true joy is readily available.

70
DON'T JUDGE THE PRESENT BY THE PAST

You cannot judge your present circumstance
by your past experiences.
Do not live your hurts,
projecting them onto innocent people.
So many carry their wounds and past hardships with them wherever they go.
The weight of these energies cloud their ability to see clearly what is in front of them.
They are stuck in their perceptions,
believing that everyone is out to hurt them
as someone once did.

Choose not to live in this way.
Your experiences matter,
yet surely you have grown, changed, and learned
from your past;
you are better equipped to create
and to respond to your present situation.
Use discernment and protect yourself
against those who would do you harm.
Let the past help you in this way.

However, open your mind to new possibilities.
Embrace your growth and realize that you are capable
of magnetizing into your life
new energies of loving and supportive people.
Do not let the past keep your heart closed.
Open it to love.

Live fully in this present moment.
Expect better things and, by doing so,
free yourself to create them.

71
MAKE GRATITUDE YOUR ATTITUDE

Gratitude is easy
when you're surrounded with abundance
and loved ones.
When things are going well and easily,
thankfulness flows.
Yet true gratitude is not based on externals.
It is not reserved for an occasion,
nor should it be held back
until certain things align in your life.
It is an acceptance that everything in your World
is part of your spiritual journey,
leading back to the realization
of your connection to the Divine.

When you begin to hold gratitude for everything in your life,
even the undesired,
you step into a space
of connectedness with your Soul.
Your Spirit came into this life to experience,
to learn, and to grow,
and it holds dear
every opportunity for these things.
Through acceptance and appreciation
of all aspects of your life,
you align your lower and higher selves
and come into Divine Grace.

Therefore, make gratitude your attitude—your way of life.
Choose to be thankful, always, and happiness will be soon to follow.

72

BRING JOY TO LIFE

Be enthusiastic about your pursuits.
Regardless of your tasks and obligations,
be fully present and enjoy whatever it is that you must do,
in spite of circumstance or situation.
Likewise, search out that which sets your Soul ablaze
and direct as much time and energy as you are able
into that identity.

Bring joy to life.
Discover its challenges and lessons.
Delve into the hardships and the rewards that come from it.
Though your true identity will not always be accepted or validated, live it anyway.
Dive as deeply into that which makes your Spirit rejoice
as you possibly can.

Make time.
Spend money.
Accept sacrifices.
Be prepared for others not to understand.
Give yourself to your joy
and allow it to direct your path.

Give yourself permission to honor your own expression,
your own truth, just as much as you would honor an outer obligation.
.
Do not waste time begrudging your situation.
Decide to be happy with where you are
while consciously moving toward where you want to be.
Do all these things with as much exuberance as possible.
By bringing joy to your endeavors,
you will fuel them with the energy of success.

73

STICK TO THE PLAN

Don't let small things undo you.
Learn to take things in stride by not over-dramatizing
or lingering on the inconveniences of life.
Too many times focus, motivation, and attitude
are stolen by the most minor of interruptions.
Once this has happened,
it becomes easy to fall into a negative spiral of events.
Your focus on what is wrong creates an energy of negativity
and the next bad thing will be soon to follow.
Things may not time out conveniently.
People will attempt to distract you.
Plans will change.

Don't let inconveniences become excuses
to let go of your ambitions or to lose your good mood.
Be prepared to adjust your plans instead of abandoning them entirely.

Deal actively with what you must
and move past it gracefully,
so that you can resume your goals.
Do not give situations power over your attitude or focus.
Use these to redirect yourself back to the greater picture of your life.
Empower yourself in this way
and you'll see your highest goals
through to completion.

Whether they be about your relationships
or personal ambitions,
make decisions and take actions
that accord with your heart and mind here and now.

Many allow fear, insecurity, guilt, and lack of ambition
to stop them from forging new pathways in life.
They sacrifice their future happiness
for present complacency.
They grow old
wishing they had done things differently.
This need not be so.

However, you cannot hope to have a different experience later
if you do not act differently in the now.
The first step is to come into understanding of your own Self.
Find quiet times to ask your own heart's desires.

Find where you need to make peace in your life and do so.
Make learning what gives you joy in life a priority.
Likewise, find your inner limitations.
Put time, energy, and effort
into what you discover on both counts.
Do not be reckless, but do be bold in seeking happiness.

Be diligent and driven in this pursuit.
In doing so, you will create a life free of regrets
and filled with great happiness.

75

ACCEPT AND RESPECT

Some people will not like or understand
your choices or actions.
Likewise, you will find some
whom you do not agree with or care for.
In all such instances,
keep your focus on respect and acceptance.

Many people fall into unnecessary conflict with others
because of differences:
instead of seeking common ground,
they focus only on what doesn't match their truth.
Some try to force others into agreeing with them
or to acting in a certain way.
By coercing others into agreement,
they feel they have validated their own truth.
Instead, they have simply created distance
and hurt by invalidating another's personal expression.

People have a right to their own way of being.
Celebrate diversity, but do not give up your truth.

To honor another's path is to honor
the creative aspect of Spirit and,
thereby, your own Soul.
Give freely to others the acceptance you desire
and free yourself from needless conflict.
Be yourself and allow the same for others.

76
GIVE UP GOSSIP

Gossiping is of a very low vibration
and is an insult to the Soul.
Do not allow yourself to create or participate
in damaging stories about others.
The soul craves truthful expression
and to speak otherwise hurts your own Self
far more than it harms anyone else.
Fitting in is simply not worth what you lose in exchange.
You'll be known as untrustworthy and small-minded.
Your integrity will wither in the eyes of others.

It can be a challenge to refuse when others choose negative talk,
but it is the mark of one on an enlightened path.
Likewise, give no power to the stories
and gossip others would spread about you.
Give no energy whatsoever to such things.

Allow the truth of your being to be so evident
that it needs no defense.
Do not allow another person's words about you
to prompt you to respond and drag you into their negativity.
Rise above it and stand comfortably in your truth,
knowing that it will endure
as your real identity.

Remove gossips from your life and surround yourself
with those of a higher nature.
Be a guardian of truth.

77

FEEL FULLY—AND THEN LET GO

Emotions are powerful energies
that should not be suppressed.
They are meant to be felt.
So many people attempt to limit or deny their emotions
to preserve a sense of self-control.
They suffer in attempting to keep an appearance of composure
or to hide the truth of how they feel.
This is a disservice to the Self and to those in a person's life.

Your Soul came into this body so that you could experience the World
and the lessons you need to grow.
How can this be done when emotions are denied?

In remembering moments from your past,
it is how you felt that will stick with you the most.
When faced with an emotional situation, step into your feelings.
Granted, you should take others into consideration
and not inflict your emotions on them.
To do so is manipulative and selfish.
However, you should find time to step fully into your feelings
and allow whatever real response comes from within to rise to the surface.

Instead of repressing your emotions, embrace them.
When faced with a powerfully emotional situation,
take a moment to release your feelings completely.
Cry, laugh, scream—whatever is appropriate and matches how you feel.
Then, gather yourself and choose your next steps.

In this way, you will honor your feelings
and allow yourself to choose wise actions.

78
LEARN TO LAUGH AT YOURSELF

Find humor
in your circumstances whenever possible.
Do not take yourself so seriously, clinging desperately
to self-image and self-imposed
ideas of perfection.
Laugh instead.

Free yourself from pressure
and burden with joy and mirth.
A little silliness can be therapeutic.
Yes, you will make mistakes.
You will at times look foolish.
At other times you will simply be wrong.
Accept these things with good humor
and let go of judgment and self-punishment.

No doubt that there are serious matters
to which this will not apply,
but finding humor whenever possible
is a gift to your Soul.

Learn to laugh and embrace yourself,
flaws, awkwardness, and all.
Let your stumbles become a dance.
Let your misspoken words
become part of a funny song.

Laugh as freely as a child
and you will become happy and light,
regardless of your circumstances.

79
BE BOLD WITH YOUR AMBITIONS

Realize here and now
that you are capable of far more
than you have allowed yourself to believe.
Do not let society's demands for conformity
limit your creative ability.
Be different.

Within you, buried under the doubts,
fears, and criticisms from others, lies a pure creative force
imbued by Spirit with the power of expression.
Envision greatness in your life and then take great steps to make it so.
Gather around you individuals that support
and validate your desires for self-expression.

Begin to see every obstacle and challenge
as redefining moments instead of stopping points.
Take the time and energy usually devoted to fear
and anxiety, and redirect it into motivation and action.

Do not give up easily.
Do not allow others to pull you away from your truth
with their own disbelief or judgments.
Dig deep within yourself, find your true joy, and devote your life to it.
Be tireless in your pursuit.

Decide today that you deserve to be happy
and give what is inside of you a chance to be shared fully with the World.
Let your light shine and watch the darkness fade from your life.

80
EMBRACE YOUR UNIQUENESS

For many people,
not feeling accepted
is the worst thing that can happen to them.
In reality, it is far worse to be accepted under false pretenses
than to stand alone in your truth.
The desire to fit in will push many people to deny their own expression
and alter their appearance, actions,
and even beliefs for the sake of gaining acceptance.
The opinion of others will push them into reactions
and they will lose themselves in the expectations of others.
To do this is to deny your Soul's expression.
Your uniqueness is a gift from Spirit.
What makes you different is what makes you great.
The grandest accomplishment is to show one's uniqueness to the World.
When you meet someone who has embraced this,
you will notice an aura of confidence and magnetism around them.
They will seem to have a connection to the Divine
that is reflected in their choices and actions.

Decide today to be one of these people.
Find the blessing of difference within you that Spirit
has gifted you with and then work tirelessly to give it expression.
Free your truth into the World.
Through this, people who validate and cherish your uniqueness
will gather around you as kindred Spirits,
offering you support and celebrating with you the voice of your truth.
When you accept yourself you will find
the acceptance you seek from others.
To be fully you is to be fully blessed.

81
LEARN PATIENCE

Many disappointments and frustrations in life
can be avoided by developing patience.
Many opportunities are missed
because individuals get so wrapped up
in their own sense of timing and urgency
that they cannot accept the natural unfolding of events.
It is a belief that what you want and when you want it
matters more than anyone or anything else.
Much suffering and aggravation
will be found in this approach to life.

However, when you develop patience,
believing that everything is happening as it should,
and when you trust that Spirit is working in ways
that you may not even be aware of,
your life will become flowing and graceful.
You will find that other people's urgencies no longer affect you.
You will find peace within yourself,
even when putting great efforts into changing your life.

Slow down and enjoy the process and fullness
of whatever experience you are having.
Decide to not let the hurried and expectant energy
of others dictate your pace.
Patience and Faith work hand in hand.

Being patient with yourself is a sign
that you are on the path of Enlightenment.
Being patient with others is a sign of
one who has chosen happiness.

82
LEAD BY EXAMPLE

Be an inspiration to others.
Make this your way of being in good times and in bad.
Regardless of your challenges and circumstances, in fact because of them,
you have the power to be inspirational to someone else.
It does not matter nearly so much what is happening in your life
as it does how you respond to it.
Some people in your World will benefit greatly
from remembering this.
Remind them with your actions.
Lead by example.

Instead of giving into the negatives in your life,
decide to rise above them.
Exhibit so much faith and diligence
that others around you notice.
Become a force of positive changes in your own life,
never giving up on your quest
for betterment.

Flow gracefully along the troubled waters of life.
Refuse to participate in mindless complaints
and let go of the need for the World to share in your burdens.
Learn to look past what is wrong
and give all your energy toward the remedies
rather than the problems.
This is one of the greatest gifts
that you can give to yourself
and to the World.

83

HAVE FAITH IN DARK TIMES

You will be faced with dark times in your life.
You will find yourself questioning your choices
and may even wonder if what you have held
with so much value in your life has any worth at all.
In these moments, you must have faith.
You must realize there is a higher power
at work in your life and that you are connected to
that source of all things.
The entire Universe is in a constant state of change
and yet every piece, every tiny bit of it,
flows together in a great interconnected symphony of expression.
Everything fits together.

How then could you believe your life to be otherwise?
When you become disconnected from your awareness
that you are indeed part of the Divine,
that your Soul is experiencing exactly what is right for it,
you will have doubt and sorrow.
You will experience an emptiness
that will hold you in sadness like a prison.

However, when you live fully present in the circumstance of your life,
trusting that all is as it should be,
you will have stepped into faith
and the freedom that comes with it.

Do not succumb to the doubt and loss of faith
that can come with hard times.
Let these moments push you further into Spiritual trust.
Let faith be a real force in your life.

84
AVOID OTHER PEOPLE'S DRAMATICS

Do not allow yourself to be
pulled into the pettiness of others.
People will try to draw you into their issues
and may even bait you into agreement
in an effort to validate their own thoughts and feelings.
Some people obsess over the tiniest of situations,
making them seem monumental.
Others will become fixated on situations
that have absolutely nothing to do with them.
They will rant and preach
and become overly emotional.

Rise above this way of being.
Give your time and energy
to those things that truly matter.
Reclaim your thoughts,
pulling them away from unnecessary things.
Establish boundaries and do not be afraid to say you will not participate
in lower conversations or hysterics.
Choose not to enter into the pointless arguments or complaints,
for when you do, you will have given away your power.
Your energy will feed someone else's drama
instead of creating a better World for yourself.

Become a force for good in the World
and channel your efforts into real actions instead of dramatic exchanges.
This is the path of the enlightened
that leads to a better personal experience in life and
real changes that benefit humanity.

85
REVEL IN KIND WORDS

Do not turn away
the kind words of others.
They are gifts to be treasured.
Many people feel undeserving of praise
and will deflect compliments or kind attentions.
They will feign humility to mask their insecurity about themselves
and hold onto a negative self-image
instead of welcoming another's higher view of them.
This is unfortunate, as it robs both people of potential happiness.

Do not deny others the happiness
that comes with offering compliments.
Likewise, know that what others see in you
may be more accurate than your own self-image.
Open yourself to the positive comments of others.
Let their uplifting words do exactly that.

Be welcoming and appreciative,
especially when you feel undeserving.
When someone compliments you,
their Soul is trying to remind you of the grand truth
that all are deserving of love and acceptance.

Also, do not withhold your praise.
Be complimentary whenever possible.
When you learn to give and take in this way,
you have chosen to be both blessed yourself
and a blessing to others.
This is the true nature of your Spirit.

86
CREATE POSITIVE ENERGY

Let your focus
be on what is good in the World.
There will be problems and challenges that you must face,
but, even in these moments,
allow yourself to focus on solutions
instead of giving energy to what is wrong.
When you focus on negatives you fuel them to become
even more present in your life.
You reinforce your connections to them
instead of realigning yourself
with something better.

Your energy goes where your focus is placed.
What you believe and expect
is what you will experience in life.
Therefore, you must retrain your mind
to be directed always toward good.
Let go of the need to give constant voice to your problems
through complaint and oversharing.

Do not let your burdens be your identity.
Instead, rise above each and every problem
by seeing it as an opportunity to grow
and gain experience.

Think, speak, and act in positive ways.
When you take all of your attention and energy away from negativity,
your life will become an expression of joy.
Place your attention on good, and your life will respond in kind.

87
BUILD A POSITIVE SELF-IMAGE

Be diligent
in weeding out negative thoughts
or comparisons to others.
Let go of the criticisms others have placed upon you.
These are poisons that destroy happiness.
Build a positive self-image.
Let yourself be grand and magnificent.
You are a Soul, made of love and light,
capable of amazing things.
Do not let your personal reflections of Self
be any less amazing.
Validate your identity, your accomplishments,
and even your struggles.
They are uniquely yours and are all expressions
of the Divine Dance called life.

By adopting a positive self-image,
you radiate an energy of Creation.
This same energy will flow back to you in abundance.
Love yourself and others will as well.

Validate yourself
and the World will begin to acknowledge you
in ways you had only hoped for before.

88
DON'T EXPECT OTHERS TO CHANGE

See all people as they are instead of how you want them to be.
Decide to cast off the illusions brought on by denial and false hopes.
So many suffer because they form bonds with people based on their own desires,
instead of accepting them as they really are.

Countless opportunities for happiness are lost in hoping
that someone you care for will love you enough to change.
Instead, you should move on to someone
who fits your life without needing to change.
Potential friendships are lost because they don't match up to your expectations.

Therefore, wipe away expectations.
Use discernment when it comes to the people you share your time with.
Learn to accept people as they are, instead of how you would wish them to be.
It is better to let go of someone, honoring their truth
even though it differs from your own,
than to hold a false image in your mind
over the truth of their expression.

Seek out individuals who fit your personality and your life
just as they are, and let go of the need to change others.
You will find the happiness you seek through truth and acceptance.
You will find freedom in honesty with yourself.

89
LET GO OF COMPARISONS

Your life is a beautiful expression,
not a contest.
There will always be those with greater and lesser wealth.
Focusing on possessions—whether one's own or others'—
will never bring happiness.
Neither will comparison to others
who you feel are more attractive
or physically blessed in some way.
Likewise, you will suffer when you are jealous
of the accomplishments of others.
Free yourself from such burdens by letting go of comparisons.

Be quick to celebrate the successes of others.
Be the first to offer congratulations and compliments.
Enjoy the beauty in everyone you meet
while thriving in your own uniqueness.
It is only when you have gratitude for what you have
that your life becomes meaningful.
Strive for contentment with what you have in life.

You are a Divine being, a Soul placed in this physical World
for the sole purpose of self-expression.
Why then would you spend time worrying about what others are doing,
what they look like, or even what they think?

Seek joy and celebrate your own expression.
Your life is a gift, unique and amazing.
Do not take away from that by comparisons.
Decide to let go of the competition
and you will have already won.

90
BE INSPIRED BY CREATION

Allow yourself to be awed and inspired
by the wonder of Creation all around you.
Begin to see the entire World as a grand expression of Spirit.
Let even the smallest of things be as a miracle in your eyes.
Choose to see the beauty and grandeur of life
as a reflection of that which is inside of you.
Let this awareness ignite within you the power
to create the experiences you desire.

The sole purpose of all things,
both blessings and hardships,
are to lead you back to the awareness that you are a part of Spirit
and that you have the ability to re-create your experience
at any moment through faith, intention, and action.
When you allow yourself to realize
that you are connected to all things,
you will see that what you want
is already a part of your World.

When you do not see yourself or your life as connected in this way,
you will suffer difficulties and sadness.
Everywhere there will be obstacles.
However, when you accept all that is
as part of a great interconnected truth,
you have stepped into a sacred awareness that grants freedom
of personal expression and joy.

The key to lasting happiness is the realization that you are
a Divine being capable of limitless expression and creation,
free to rewrite your story at any time.

91
SHOW GRATITUDE

One of the most harmful things you can do
is to take someone for granted.
It is a selfish mindset that steals others' self-esteem.
It keeps you from experiencing deeper connections with others.
Even when love is present, relationships are damaged
or lost when one individual is unable to show the other
consideration and caring.

Practice appreciation and gratitude on a constant basis.
Seek to be humble, just as you seek to be strong.
The two go hand in hand.
Tell the people you care about how you feel.
More importantly, show them.

For your own well-being, be self-focused when needed,
but become selfless at other times.
Give as freely as you receive.

When you bless another person with your time,
gratitude, and caring, you have given yourself a monumental gift.
You have reconnected with your true nature.
Be thankful for those in your life.
You have chosen for them to be there.

Your Soul sings a constant song
of love and gratitude.
When you open yourself to it,
it rings through your entire life, uplifting all who hear it.

92

CHOOSE YOUR REALITY

The experiences of your life radiate from deep within
your own consciousness.
Everything you are aware of,
both the good and the bad,
are echoes of your own energies.

Life is not happening to you.
It is happening through you.
Understanding this empowers you
to make real and lasting changes in your life.

Many distance themselves from their own inner thoughts,
closing off feelings from previous experiences
in an attempt to control in their mental state.
Dissociated from the energies they send into the World,
they find their days filled with chaos.
The emotions they try so hard to ignore
begin to dictate their thoughts, choices, and actions—
all of which creates their future experiences.

Choose instead to embrace your inner thoughts.
Connect with what you really feel inside.
Strive to understand your emotions
and shift your thoughts to match what you wish to create.
Become diligent in seeing your outer World as a reflection of your inner Self.

You are the root cause of all your joys and sorrows.
Own this and you will become empowered
with choices over your reality.

93
SPEAK OUT AGAINST WRONGS

To realize something is wrong and do nothing about it
makes you part of the problem.
Be proactive in making the World a better place.
If this isn't your responsibility, then whose is it?
Speak out!

Yes, people have the right to express themselves
and to live in their own truth.
It is vastly important to honor this.
However, that right ends
when it brings harm to another.

There are many who disrespect boundaries
and manipulate others for their own agendas.
Some will even steal things outright.
Small-minded individuals will speak in ways that tear others down.
Unfortunately, some do not know how others should be treated;
even worse, some know and do not care.

Do not stand for these wrongs
when you have the ability to right them.
Speak out for the children and animals
that cannot protect themselves.
Come to the rescue of those in need.
Establish and defend personal boundaries and truths.

Be a voice and a force for good in all areas of your life.
Decide today that you will no longer be complacent
and allow negativity a foothold in your World.
Become a champion, a hero to all of humanity.

94
LISTEN TO YOUR INNER VOICE

The path of Spirit leads inward, not outward.
Glimpses of the Divine that you see in your outer World
are reflections of what is inside of you.
Each of the World's religions will tell you it alone possesses truth.
At times, it will seem there is only a single narrow path that leads to Spirit.
A great many people will tell you this is so.
This cannot be true.

The Divine lives within every man, woman, and child on this Earth.
Every person is unique and individual.
Therefore, every Path
is individual, personal, and sacred.

Every moment of your life is designed
to push you back to this inner path.
Every hardship is meant to turn you to seek faith.
Every blessing is a reminder of the joys that faith brings.
True faith teaches that you are part of something grander
than yourself and that there is a reason for everything.
When you seek a place of worship, look into a mirror
and see the beautiful temple your Soul has been residing in.
Establish the religion of compassion as your outer expression,
but always return to the inner path.

Practice the religion of Self.
Let your life be a reflection of the Divinity within you
and your World will be filled
with happiness, understanding, and love.

95
LOOK FOR BEAUTY

The Soul craves beauty,
for it reminds it of its truest essence.
It is part of the great Oneness of all things.
It is an expression of the Divine,
and it is the part of you that is radiant light and love.
It is the force of Creation expressing itself in physical form.

Do not allow yourself to forget these truths.
Seek out beauty in this World as a reminder to the Self
that you are part of something amazing and wonderful.
Look for the beauty of Spirit in every face you see.
Let each opening flower be a reflection of your own awareness unfolding.
Hear the voice of Spirit in a child's laughter.
Welcome all of Creation into your senses
and let it fill you with a sense of belonging.

Allow all that you encounter to become voices in a grand chorus,
rising into one amazing harmony.
By reveling in the wonders that surround you,
you will have stepped onto the path of enlightenment.

Therefore, let the rains cleanse your Soul
and the sun bathe you in its light.
Let the expansiveness of a starry night
remind you of the grandeur of your own Spirit.
When you begin to see beauty in everything,
you will come to see the Divine and, indeed,
your own higher Self.

96
MAKE A DIFFERENCE

Intolerance, hate, poverty, greed, and destruction of the land
are but a few of the negative energies that face humanity daily.
Many would look at the World and wish it were better;
however, few are willing actually to do anything about it.
They may want things to be different but refuse to change personally
or be a voice for that change,
out of fear of falling victim to rejection.
Many people are too selfish to care about things
that affect others and not themselves.
To live within this mindset is to deny the truth of your existence.
All things are connected on a Soul level.
What happens to others does indeed happen to a part of you.
What you do personally and what you allow in your presence
define you as an individual
and dictate your future experiences.
Do not give in to complacency, selfishness, cynicism, or despair.

Allow kindness and compassion to fuel real actions for change in your World.
Become a force for positive changes wherever you are able.
Begin with what is right in front of you.
Take up a cause: give time, money, effort toward helping others.
Speak out against those who would harm others
or hold others down in life, even when this makes you unpopular.
Become a selfless force of good in the World.

You have far more power than you believe.
Become a blessing unto others
and you will become blessed
within your own life.

97

SEEK SELF-MASTERY

Accomplishment is an amazing feeling.
Setting goals and reaching them gives you a sense of freedom and empowerment.
Your Soul will seek changes for betterment in your life
and will urge you toward transformation.
By listening to yourself and following through with your intentions and goals,
you will be honoring your Soul's desire
and will find happiness and satisfaction.

Unfortunately, many people deny themselves these feelings
by giving into distractions or, worse,
by allowing obstacles to stop them in their pursuits entirely.
They will give up because what they seek
is difficult or requires investments of time and effort.
Some will even feel unworthy of positive changes in their lives,
allowing insecurities to block forward movement.

Take time to listen to your higher Self.
Allow that inner voice to inspire your intentions and goals.
Then, become relentless in their pursuit.

Surround yourself with people who encourage and support your efforts.
Decide today that there is no obstacle greater than your will,
no distraction greater than your focus,
and nothing that will keep you from the happiness of success.
Give nothing outside of you the power to stop you.
Likewise, give nothing inside your own Self that power to stop you.

Once you commit to change, you will be able to step into the joy
that comes with perseverance and accomplishment.

98

WED EMOTIONS TO REASON

So many people make poor choices
because they react from emotion rather than reason.
They allow their feelings to dictate their response to the World.
Some allow fear, insecurity, doubt, or some other lower emotion
to stop them from doing what they know is best.
Others will overreact and, in their zeal, will overreach in pursuing their desires,
their presumed happiness, or even love.

Your emotions are meant to inform you.
They are to help you understand the experiences you are going through.
They help you to define your circumstance
but are not meant to dictate your actions.
Do what is right instead of reacting to what you feel.
Allow your emotions and reason to combine:
step into a space of wisdom and, from this place,
choose your next steps wisely.

When you find balance between what you know
and what you feel, you will empower yourself to make right choices.
Each experience you have will prepare you for the next,
and you will find it easy to do what is best for you.

Allow the feelings you have to deepen your experiences and understanding,
but do not give them the power to dictate your choices and actions.
When you discover the ability to balance emotions and reason,
you will experience a happier and more productive life.

99
ACCEPT WHAT IS

Learn to live in acceptance of the things you cannot change.
Many disappointments in life stem from refusing to accept things as they are,
holding on to how you would have them be.
Individual preferences and expectations do not always align with reality,
and things do not always go as planned.
This is natural, and yet it seems impossible for some to accept.
They will continue to put great focus and effort toward what they want,
even after it is evident that it is not going to come into being.

This can be especially true of relationships.
The desire to have another act and respond
as you would want them to can lead to deep disappointment.
Only when you accept them as they are can that person comfortably fit into your life.
When someone does not match your truth,
bless them and yourself by limiting your interactions
rather than trying to change them.

Change only for yourself and ask nothing more of those you allow into your life.
Strive for change, for personal growth and greatness,
but also learn to accept things as they are
when it becomes evident that they are not going to change.
By balancing expectation and acceptance in your life,
you will step into an energy of empowerment
rather than one of wasted efforts.
Be the change, even if than means changing your own perspective.
When you live in acceptance, you live in peace.
What greater blessing could there be?

100

VALUE EFFORT OVER OUTCOME

As you grow older,
you will look back on your life in one of two ways.
You will look back with regret over the things you never did,
or with satisfaction over the attempts you made.
This will be regardless of the outcomes in either case.

It is rarely the actual accomplishment that the Soul craves.
It is the willingness of the Self to cast off limitations
and step into experience.

The true joy of life comes from breaking out of fear and self-doubt
and giving action to that which is inside of you.
So many allow opportunities for self-expression pass them
through of fear of failure or of not being accepted by others,
should they be successful.
They allow self-doubt to stop them from doing.
They become locked in a mental prison,
wondering what might have been.

What you do today will form what you experience tomorrow.
Do not allow your life to pass by without giving yourself permission to do
what is within you to do.

Start today to build the memories
that you will savor in your old age.
Give every action in your life meaning and,
at the end of your days,
you will have lived a meaningful life.

101

HELP YOURSELF BY HELPING OTHERS

Showing compassion even while enduring your own hardships
is a sign of integrity and character.

While your own challenges may be hard,
they are not all there is in the World.
Some, however, wear their troubles like a badge of honor.
You will not have to wonder what is happening in their lives,
as they will tell you over and over.
They fixate on their problems until that is all there is to them.
They will become so entrenched in their thoughts
that no one or nothing else will matter to them.
Their negativity will bind them to their problems
and keep them from Self-fulfillment.

When you let go of your attachment to your problems
and quit feeding them energy, they will begin to fade.
Being selfless is a powerful tool for change.

When you reach out with kindness and help to others,
you create a positive energy that will flow through the life of those you befriend—
and through your own life as well.

When you are faced with a problem and do not know how to fix your own life,
lay your burden down for a while.
Focus on helping someone else.
Pull the energies of worry and frustration away from your mind
by being in service to those in need.
Decide that your hardships do not own you.
They are not your identity.

Do not give them power to dictate your response to the people around you.
Choose to help others and you will find a freedom and happiness beyond words.
Your troubles will fade and your light will shine through.

102
SPEAK YOUR TRUTH

Make truth your way of being.
Live it, speak it, demand it.
Being honest in your expression is the greatest sign of respect
you can show for yourself and others.
To live within your truth means to be who you are
fully and without apology.

Cast away fear of not being appreciated or accepted and,
short of harming or hindering another, just be yourself.
Allow the identity you hold inside of you to become your outer expression.
Be bold and brave enough to show the World who you really are.

Likewise, speak your truth.
People who take a higher path will always speak in honesty,
but will offer kindness and compassion in their delivery.
Do not withhold the truth from those around you.
Be honest even if the other person wants to hear something other than your truth.
By doing this you will form real, lasting relationships.
People will come to know and respect you
for your honesty and insights.

Demand that same degree of truth and honesty
from those you allow into your life.
Question that which you know to be untrue.
Set an expectation of honesty within your circle
and be diligent about that demand.
Make it well known that you require people to mirror
the respect you show them through your honesty.
Do not tolerate those who lie and mislead,
even those who claim it is for a good reason.

Make truth the standard for your entire life
and you will be blessed with happiness and liberation.
You will also become a powerful force
for change in the World.

103
SLOW YOUR PACE

Do not rush through your life
as though you were running a race.
Getting to the end is not the same in life
as it is in a contest.

Too many people hurry from one moment in life to the next.
They proclaim how busy they are, as though this were an accomplishment in itself.
They rush through events of their lives like checklists, moving from task to task
without pausing to savor their accomplishments.

These same people may suffer from feeling that others do not validate their efforts
when they themselves—through their own hectic pace—
leave no room for validation or praise.
Some will find themselves retracing steps
and repeating actions that were poorly attended to, due to haste.
The saddest moments are those of pure joy, of the beautiful happenings of life,
that are lost when people look ahead to their next tasks,
without savoring the present moment.

Do not allow yourself to live this way.
Slow down, both internally and in your outer actions.
Calm your thoughts and approach your activities
within this same state of calmness.

Learn the difference between true life urgencies
and urgencies that are self-imposed.
Be protective of your time and always leave room for relaxation,
reflection, and just being.

When you approach life with a slower pace,
you will find treasures in this World
that would have passed
unnoticed before.

104

LET GO OF THE PAST

Learn to let go of the things that no longer serve you.
Too many people fail to move forward
by giving all their energy to what once was—
to past hurts and even to self-inflicted obstacles
that exist only within their own minds.
By focusing on what is, or has been, wrong,
they infuse an energy of negativity into everything they do.
Often this paralyzes them and they become unable to do anything at all.
These people will often return to their hurts and challenges
in every conversation, every exchange.

Let go of the obligation
to indulge this type of interaction.
Accept that you cannot change the past and that only by letting go of it
will you be free to create a better future.
Forgive yourself and others for past choices and actions.
Move on from everything that serves no purpose in your life.
Choose not to allow others to take you to a bad place in your mind.
Take quiet time of introspection to weed out the limiting thoughts
brought on by past experiences.
Simply decide to give these no more power.

This will free your energy and focus
so that you can create the life you desire.
It is only when you let go of what was that you
become free to create what will be.

Your future is yet to be written.
Focus on the story you are creating
instead of the one you've already read,
and you will become the author
of your own destiny.

105
TAKE TIME FOR SILENCE

Invest in quiet time each day.
By taking times of silence
you will learn to hear your inner thoughts and your higher Self.
Many people are so uncomfortable with their own inward identity
that they distract themselves with noise and activity.
They will reflect this in their interactions with others,
never finding comfort in silence.
They become nervous and unable to sit still
when there is nothing happening around them.
They will talk with no purpose or reason, but just to fill the quiet.
This keeps their interactions with others at a surface level.

This is unfortunate, because they miss out on the deeper connection
that comes in quiet moments.

Find comfort in silence when interacting with others, especially those you hold dear.
Learn to listen and let go of the need to control the direction of conversation.

Allow yourself to become quiet within and you will begin to hear your true inner thoughts.
Some of these will be uncomfortable and opportunities for growth.
Some will not even be your own thoughts.
They will be imprints left by others.
It is only through silent introspection
that you can begin to change these patterns
and truly understand yourself.

This is the moment of true blessing.

Your Soul is constantly guiding and directing you toward your truth.
By taking quiet times and listening to this inner voice,
you will be led to your real expression, your true path,
and gain a happiness
you have never known before.

106

CHOOSE TO BELIEVE

The entire Universe is reaching out to you.
It is guiding you toward your Soul's true expression.
When pondering your purpose in life,
look for that which strikes a deep, resonant chord within you.
Spirit is speaking to you through every possible means:
when you open yourself to that knowledge,
you will begin to see everything in your World as a roadmap
leading you to your Soul's purpose.
By recognizing the repeating patterns in your life,
you will be shown the lessons you need to learn,
the direction your path should follow,
and the truth of your purpose.

It becomes easy for some to forget this.
They will wander through life, proclaiming that nothing makes sense.
They will claim coincidence rather than allow everything
to have meaning and purpose.
They will avoid taking control of their lives by clinging to this notion.
Living in this way diminishes your connection to the Divine.
It clouds the awareness of something grander
than mere physical existence and robs you of the wonder
of the miracles happening around you.

Choose to believe.
Let your faith grow through the acceptance
that everything is connected and that everything in your life,
all you encounter, is showing you the direction
you should take to find happiness and fulfillment.
You are a part of all that is.
You have a purpose.

Open your awareness and let all of Creation
reflect the truth of your Soul to you.
This is living in Grace.

107
RE-CREATE YOURSELF

Do not try to fix what is wrong.
In doing so, you are aligning yourself with the problem.
Instead, give all of your energy to positive thoughts and actions.
Many negative situations will seem difficult to resolve
and may become greater problems when you focus on them.
By putting your attention on what is wrong,
you are feeding it energy and allowing it a place in your mind
and your World.

You have the power to re-create yourself and your experiences.
By placing your energy and focus on what you desire,
knowing it is possible through faith,
you will begin to align yourself
with positive changes in your life.

When something is not right in your World,
acknowledge it and then turn your attention toward solutions only.
Focus on how you want things to be and take whatever real actions
you can toward making them that way.
Allow your inner and outer dialogue be about
what is right and good in your life.
Focus with gratitude on having the life you choose for yourself
and pour everything you have into that reality.

Know that where you place your attention determines
what you will experience in this life,
and use this knowledge to create happy
and satisfying existence.

108
BE YOURSELF, NOT YOUR SITUATIONS

Do not let circumstances define you.
Regardless of what is happening in your life,
remember that you alone define who you are.
Only you know your reasons and motivations
for your choices and actions.
Others may try to cast you in a certain light
because of your past or present situations.
They may judge you for your responses to life,
not knowing the full story.
They will look only at the surface,
never understanding the truth of your identity that lies within.
In this same way, many people will only value themselves
according to society's expectations.

You are a beautiful Soul.
You are made of light and love.
You are the embodiment of Creation.
When presented with challenges, go within
and remember you have the power
to redefine yourself in any given moment.
You are not bound by your past,
your obstacles, or what others think of you.
None of these things matter to your Soul-Self.

When you respond to your World from this awareness,
you step into Divine Grace and will begin to change your experience.
This new-found freedom will allow you
to define your life instead of its defining you.
Be yourself, not your situations.
Remember your truth,
no matter how hard others try to make you forget it.
This is the key to lasting happiness.

109
LEARN TO LET GO

In life, there are times to hold on and times to let go.
People and situations will come into your life for a reason.
They will leave your life for a reason, as well.
By releasing the old from your life, you create space for new experiences.
Unfortunately, many people hold on to outmoded thoughts.
They repeat familiar patterns in their lives, even when
it is evident to others around them that it is time for change.
Some hold tightly to negative relationships.
The fear of being alone, or insecurities about being loved,
will keep them trapped in unfulfilling relationships.
Others may miss opportunities in life because these are not familiar.
They will hold desperately to what they know, even if it isn't what they really want.
Choose not to be limited in this way.

Have faith.
Trust Spirit and trust yourself.
When a situation has served its purpose in your life,
allow it to fade away while holding gratitude for the gift it has given you.
By recognizing that a relationship has run its course,
no matter how grand it was in its beginning,
honor yourself and the other person by letting go and stepping away.

Freedom is not being bound or limited.
It is about trusting that there is something better
and believing in your own ability to re-create your life.
The situations and people in your life should be there
because you want them there and because they benefit you,
not because you are holding on out of familiarity or sentiment.
Trust that by letting go you will free your energies
to create new and amazing experiences for yourself.
The only way to move forward in life
is to let go of where you are now.

110
CREATE THE WORLD YOU WANT BY THE WORDS YOU SPEAK

Your words define you.
By becoming accountable for what you say,
you step into an energy of self-mastery.
By disciplining yourself only to speak truth
and by remembering compassion while doing so,
you will be honoring your
Soul-Self while gaining the respect of those around you.

Speak your truth calmly and directly.
Think before you speak and let go of the need
to fill silence with meaningless chatter.
Become known for being thoughtful in your speech.
Do not expect others to know what you are thinking,
and do not play games with your communications.
Value the people in your life enough to speak plainly and directly to them.
Strive to overcome feelings that your opinion doesn't matter,
and give yourself permission to embrace your truth
and share it with the World.
Likewise, respond with acceptance and understanding
when others find the strength to share their truths with you.

Remember that a few kind words can change a circumstance,
just as a few harsh words can damage things in an instant.

Find the truth of your being.
Figure out who you really are and how you want to be known.
Make your words match this knowledge.
What you say matters.
Own your words and you will start to own your life
in a new and powerful way.
You will begin to create the life you want
by the words you speak.

TAKE PRIDE IN YOUR BODY

Your body is a temple in which your Soul lives.
It is one of the most sacred gifts you have been given by Spirit.
Through the senses of this body you are able to experience
all the wonders that this World holds.
You are able to express your Soul's truth
and connect with others.
You can dance, sing, create.
Some are gifted with brilliant minds.
Others hold unique physical abilities
that are simply amazing.
All are beautiful.

Begin to appreciate your own uniqueness.
Accept yourself, even the parts you'd like to change.
Spirit expresses itself in many and different ways,
regardless of shape or size, color, or age,
You are amazing and deserve to be valued and appreciated.

Take pride in your body and its appearance.
Revel in what sets you apart.
Embrace the truth that your Soul chose the perfect vehicle.
How could it be any other way?

Care for yourself in the foods you eat and strive
to keep your body healthy, active, and strong.
Remove harmful things and people from your life
out of respect for yourself.

When you see your physical self
as a Divine expression of your Soul,
then your relationship with your own self
will shift in an astounding
and empowering way.

112
LEARN FROM YOUR MISTAKES

Personal growth is not always easy
but it is always worth it.
The challenges you face in life give you opportunities
to explore yourself and gain understanding
of your true nature.

At different times in life you will experience success and failure.
Both are incredibly valuable chances to redefine yourself.
How you respond to these situations matters far more than the outcomes.
In moments of accomplishment, remain modest while also validating your victory.
Use the energy of success to push you to even greater moments of your personal evolution.
Let it build confidence within you and give you a sense of possibilities
and the motivation to act on them.
In these moments it is easy to feel good
about life and about yourself.

What then about the failures?
Value them equally with your accomplishments.

The wise person allows failure to be an education and nothing more.
Experience will give them perspective and understanding.
They will not fall into harsh judgment of themselves.
Ultimately, failure will change them, since change is the essence of growth.
They will incorporate the lessons learned
and use these to push to greater outcomes.
When a person allows mistakes to be a learning opportunity
without self-condemnation and gains real growth from the situation,
failures become a grand success.

113

EXERCISE YOUR POWER OF CHOICE

Your path is not a predetermined road.
It is where you choose to place your next footstep.
Many will choose the safety of a well-worn path
carved out by expectation and a need to make others happy.
The truly blessed will create a path where there was none before.
It will be a path that honors her or his inner truth.

You have been given the incredible gift
and the weighty responsibility of free will.
You have the power of choice—
of determining the direction your path will follow.

Your happiness or sadness results from choices you have made.
Yes, there will be situations that are beyond your control.
These will pass most easily through an attitude of acceptance on your part.
This, too, is a choice: not to give power to the situation,
but to remain centered within the Self.
By not reacting to a situation,
you are free to respond to it
as you see fit.

14

QUIT MAKING EXCUSES

Break the habit of blaming situations or,
worse, other people for your state of being.
Let go of blame toward parents, upbringing, or social status.
Break out of self-limiting thoughts and attitudes.
Quit making excuses.

Free yourself from the illusion that you have no control over your life.
Decide today that the power and responsibility are yours.
Take time to listen to your inner voice.
Form the path of your life firmly in your mind.
Give yourself permission to live your truth,
and then take every action you can to fulfill that vision.
Do everything you can as passionately as you can
every time you can to have the life you desire.

When you do this you will discover an amazing truth.
The entire Universe will respond to you differently.
Opportunities will open to you.
People will offer you support and validation.
All of Creation will reflect back to you
what you hold inside your own self.
Choose this image wisely, live it boldly,
and thrive in the expression
of your truth.

115

EMPOWER YOURSELF

Do not exaggerate your problems.
In doing so, you amplify their presence in your life.
By focusing on what is wrong
you will only tie yourself to the situation more strongly.

Many feel the need to make sure other people know of their struggles.
They will broadcast what is wrong out of fear
that others may not know what they are going through.
They are driven by feelings of inadequacy
in dealing with situations or by wishing
to gain support through sympathy.
Sadly, some will want others to fix things for them
without taking actions themselves.

Choose to let go of this way of being.
Free yourself by adopting an attitude that,
no matter what happens,
you are capable of dealing with it.

Make your problems small
and your ability to respond magnificent in your mind.
Surround yourself with supportive people who will want to help
and be there for you without coercion.
Spend time thinking and talking about what is good and right with your life
and not about the issues you face.
By letting go of exaggeration and drama
you will take power away from your problems
and put it back in its rightful place—
within your ability to re-create yourself
at any given moment.

Choose to be your solutions, not your problems,
and step into true empowerment.

116
EMBRACE THOSE WHO EMBRACE YOU

To share your true self with others
freely is a great blessing.
By finding individuals who understand and appreciate your uniqueness,
you will find comfort in your own self-expression.
Being yourself will come easily and effortlessly.

True friends will celebrate what is different about you.
They will encourage you to be yourself fully and always.
True friends will uplift and support you,
reminding you of your truth in difficult times.
Those who hold the greatest standing in your World
should be those who understand and validate you.

Therefore, do not waste your time on those
who make you feel small or unimportant.
Let go of people who harshly judge and ridicule you.
Release those who do not support your individuality.
Sadly, many people will cling to these types of people
out of a need to be liked by everyone.
They will sell themselves out and lose their individuality
in a quest for acceptance that, if gained, will be hollow.
Such acceptance will be based on a lie.

Embrace those who embrace you.
It is better to have a small circle of true friends
who understand and accept you
than to seek connections
out of fear of not being liked.

117
DO NOT RUN FROM YOUR CHALLENGES

Your challenges hold great value
for your personal growth and development.
Each difficulty gives you an opportunity to redefine yourself
and your response to the World around you.
They are, in fact, situations created by your higher self
in order to push you toward faith and awareness.
They shape your personality and expectations about life.

Many people fail to pursue their desires,
choosing to avoid the challenges associated with them.
Others will avoid responsibility for what faces them,
hoping that someone else will fix their problems.
Even more will shirk their responsibilities out of laziness and lack of motivation.
All such people are losing grand opportunities for self-growth.

When you avoid the lessons chosen for you by your Soul-Self,
these lessons will find ways to repeat in your experience.
But you can take the power away from your difficulties by confronting them directly:
only then will you be able to overcome them
and free yourself from this cycle of repetition.

See your obstacles simply as energies that you can affect and change.
Learn to own your challenges without allowing them to become your identity.
Embrace your power to overcome them.

By listening to your inner guidance
and by choosing to live in your highest truth,
know that you will prevail in whatever faces you in life.
Be an active force of change in your own World.
When you do so, your burdens
will become your blessings.

118
LEARN TO GIVE AND RECEIVE

It is a blessing to be able to give,
especially of your own time and self.
To do for others is among the noblest of actions,
particularly for those who are less fortunate.
Those who give and receive with gratitude are equally blessed,
and a wonderful energy is exchanged between those involved.
Therefore, place your goodwill and actions
where they are valued and appreciated.

Learn to accept the appreciation of others.
Invest in relationships that enrich your own life
while giving you a chance to do the same in return.

At the same time, do not allow yourself to be used selfishly by others.
The only relationships that are deserving of your time
and efforts are those that give to you as freely as you give to them.
It is only when you set this as your standard
that you will discover the joy of true friendship.

Be wary of those who would ask much and give little.
Their selfishness not only takes your time, but also steals your self-worth.
Hold greater value for yourself than to allow this to happen.

Demand balance and boundaries in your relationships.
Do not sacrifice these boundaries just to be liked.
Be free with your offerings to the World,
but not to the point where you become emptied and lost.
Hold close to those who give back to you,
and allow them to recharge your Spirit.
When you receive as freely as you give
and demand that those who hold place in your life
act in the same spirit,
you will be blessed yourself
and a blessing to others.

119
AVOID COMPLACENCY

The Universe is neither rewarding you
or punishing you.
It is simply responding to you.

Every thought, word, belief, and action that comes from you
affects the World around you.
Your attitudes and innermost thoughts
determine your experiences.
They are powerful energies of Creation.

What you truly hold inside of yourself
is exactly what you will live outwardly.
You—and no one else—are responsible for the life you live.
This is why complacency and inaction are such dangerous things.

Through complacency, people find it easy to blame others for their circumstances.
Some will claim they were never given opportunity.
Others will say that their challenges were too great to overcome.
Still more will blame the state of the World for their hardships.
Family, friends, and even Spirit will be held accountable by them for their woes.
This is not truth.

By taking ownership and responsibility for the life you create,
you are stepping into Divinity.
When you realize that everything you think,
everything you say, everything you believe, and everything
you do are the causes of your life's experience,
you will have reconnected with your truest nature.

You are a Soul, a force of pure creative energy endowed with free will.
You reward or punish yourself as you choose.
Realize this and you will have found the keys
to happiness and freedom.

120
SEE YOUR SOUL-SELF REFLECTED IN OTHERS

Everyone you encounter is a mirror
reflecting some aspect of yourself back to you.

What you notice most in others exists most strongly within you.
When confronted by someone unpleasant,
it is easiest to remove them from your life
by finding that part of you that mirrors their behavior.
You are the common thread in your encounters.

Therefore, do not separate yourself from your experiences.
By being fully present in every situation,
you can gain powerful insights about the self.
Ask within your own mind what you can learn about yourself
from every person in your life.
Honor the truth that is being shown to you with acceptance,
even if it is something you wish to change.

Let go of the tendency to avoid these truths.
Until you do so, you are robbing yourself of opportunities for redefinition.
To be successful in this, you must determine which reflections
are accurate and which are distorted.
Some mirrors are like those in a fun house,
exaggerating certain aspects out of proportion.
Others give more accurate reflections.
All are there for the sake of understanding the self.

Choose to let go of the overblown
or outdated parts of yourself.
Seek out the individuals who shine
with the same light you wish to show the World.
Surround yourself with people who reflect back to you
the better parts of yourself.
You will begin to see your
Soul-Self reflected in every face you meet.

121
KNOW THAT YOU ARE WORTHY

The very nature of the Universe is abundance.
Everything you need, want, or desire already exists within the World.
Why then do so many live without fulfillment?
It is a matter of the energies they themselves are sending into Creation.
It is said that your thoughts create your reality when, in truth,
your thoughts and beliefs align you with that which already exists.
They create your life-experience by connecting you with exterior circumstances that match
your inner expectations and self-image.

So many feel they do not deserve the things they want and therefore will never have them.
They will believe others deserve happiness in all forms but, when it comes to themselves,
their own feelings of unworthiness keep them from attaining what they want.
Others allow opportunities to slip away because they won't do what it takes
to have what they desire.
Laziness, fear, self-doubt, and feelings of undeserving
keep them from experiencing the World's abundance.

Open your mind to a new way of thinking.
Know that there is more than enough for everyone in all things.
Decide that, by Divine right, you are deserving of all you seek.
Focus on possibilities and act on every opportunity that comes your way.
Change your inner perspective of yourself
and your life and the entire World will shift to match
your newfound expression.

What you seek already exists.
You will have it the moment you decide
to accept and act on it.

122

STAND IN YOUR OWN TRUTH

When you stand for something,
even if it means standing alone,
you have given yourself definition and focus.
Not sacrificing what you know to be right is the very essence of integrity.
Give no thought to those who do not like you or what you stand for.
Also, give no effort toward change for their benefit.

When you change yourself for another person
instead of for your own self, you lose your identity.
You become defined by what is expected of you,
instead of what by you intend to put forth into the World.
The desire to be liked will begin to take hold and control your every action,
and what you truly stand for will become lost
in trying to win favor in the eyes of others.
Others' desires will begin to replace your own.

If this happens, you will find yourself lost and without identity.
Your definition will be nothing more
than an echo of those around you, lacking in individuality.

This does not mean you shouldn't do for others.
It means you should have healthy boundaries when doing so.
Be selfless in your efforts toward others,
but do not let those efforts rob you of what you believe to be right.
Learn the distinction between giving to help
without motive and trying to win favor.
Give as freely as you are able
without taking from your truth.

Living your truth is the greatest blessing
you can have.

123
DO WHAT IS RIGHT

Every person is born with a sense of right and wrong.
However, far too many people will opt for ease or complacency
instead of simply doing what is right.
They will create excuses and give the smallest obstacles the power
to stop them from living their highest good.
Even worse, some will attempt to hold others
accountable for their own bad actions.
They will place blame instead of owning the fact
that they did something wrong
or did nothing at all when there was need.
Some individuals will knowingly do wrong things
out of a desire for acceptance by others.
They will place social approval over their own integrity.

How can you expect good in your life
if you do not create good through your choices and actions?
The energies you send out will come back to you.

Therefore, choose that which is right and good.
Refuse to participate in negativity.
Let go of the people who encourage you toward wrong things.
Stand apart by deciding always to do the next right thing,
regardless of how you feel in the moment.
Embrace truth and live it so fully and with such integrity
that you inspire others.

By doing what is right, regardless of approval,
you are aligning yourself with your Soul's true expression.
You will become a champion unto yourself,
liberating your own existence
into one of light and happiness.

124

BECOME ONE WITH WHAT YOU SEEK

It is not enough simply to want something.
It is not even enough to work toward your goals.
In order to have what you want, you must become that which you desire.
If you want love in your life, you must become more loving.
When you seek truth, you must be honest yourself.
Should you desire prosperity, you have to allow yourself
to feel worth and value within.
This is the nature of all experience.

That which you are inwardly is that which you will experience outwardly.
The Universe works on a simple principle: like attracts like.

Setting intentions toward your goal
will begin to create opportunities in your World.
However, it is only when you become one with that which you seek
that the opportunities become evident.
Only then are you able to follow through
with the choices and actions that lead to attainment.

You cannot hope to experience something in your outer World
until you align with it internally.
Everything in your experience
is a reflection of what you hold inside.
No matter what it is that you want in life,
search for it first within yourself.
Establish it as your inner truth and you will begin
to magnetize the people, energies,
and opportunities necessary to experience it outwardly.
As with all things,
the key to happiness is to begin within.

125
ACCEPT PEOPLE AS THEY ARE

People will disappoint you.
This is inevitable, as is the hurt
that goes along with disappointment.
When dealing with others, you may find that your expectations
and their actions do not match.
You will trust those who do not deserve it,
love those who don't return it,
and believe things about others that prove untrue.
These lessons will leave strong impressions
and lead you to choose different boundaries and responses in the future.
The wise will accept life's lessons and grow
without letting the hurt rob them
of the ability to trust and love.

The balance between learning a lesson and becoming a victim is delicate.
Many relationships are based on possibilities rather than realities.
How people could be and how they actually are can vary widely.
Each person has free will as to how they interact with others.
Learn to accept people as they are.

Develop a sense of discernment in forming connections with others.
Take time to understand your desires and preferences,
and learn not to see others through these desires.

Become comfortable in letting go of those
who do not match you, while holding tight to those who do.
Know that you deserve those in your World
who both offer and demand truth,
while offering compassionate acceptance.
These are the people who are deserving
of your time.

126
HONOR ALL PATHS

Just as you should not change for others,
you should not expect others to change for you.
Let go of expectations and the need to control.

Allow others to be themselves fully,
free from any definitions or requirements you might wish to place on them.
Grant them the same freedom of expression that you seek for yourself.
In doing, so you will find that some people's truths do not match your own—
often to a degree that you need to free them from your life.
Others will resonate with you in ways
that complement your growth and happiness:
hold these closest to you.

Regardless of which, honor all paths, all truths.
You do not have to approve of or even share in
the journey another chooses to take.
You need only honor it.
In so doing, you honor yourself.

You will be blessed when you recognize
those on the same road you are traveling.
However, the greatest blessing will find you
when you celebrate all paths as Divine expressions.
In recognizing the freedom of others,
you embrace freedom for yourself.

127

EMBRACE COMPASSION

Living compassionately is a mark of one
who is truly on the Spiritual path.
In compassion, you elevate your own energy
along with the vibrations of the one for whom you hold it.
This World is one of lessons and growth—
which means that, at times,
you will face struggles and challenges.
Oftentimes you will be unaware of other people's struggles.
So, it is wise to be mindful that everyone
deserves your grace and understanding.

Sadly, many people criticize and condemn
another person in his or her struggles.
They judge the other person's choices and actions
while having no understanding of that person's circumstances.

To live critically this way is to deny the Spiritual understanding
that everyone, everything, everywhere is interconnected.
If one person or animal suffers, the entirety of Spirit suffers.

Let go of criticism, condemnation, and intolerance.
Free yourself from the belief that others should respond as you would,
and embrace the fact that all beings
deserve your compassion, acceptance, and love.

You cannot claim to be a loving person without practicing compassion.
When you open yourself to this understanding it will change you.
Your awareness of the interconnectedness of all things
will prompt you to take actions that better the lives of others.
In this way, the World will benefit
from your presence.

128
FORGIVE OTHERS, FORGIVE YOURSELF

When you forgive another for wrongdoing,
you free yourself from the negative energies
arising from that circumstance.
By embracing forgiveness you have liberated yourself—
regardless of what has happened—
and are free simply to learn from the situation.
You will have changed the energies of the moment,
both for yourself and for the one who wronged you.

Why then would you not apply this same understanding to yourself?
So many individuals live in regret and shame
over their own shortcomings and misdoings.
Everyone makes mistakes and wrong choices.
These are the stuff of growth and learning.

Unfortunately, many people are able to find forgiveness
for others but not for themselves.
They hold on to guilt and identify themselves by what they have done wrong.
By refusing to forgive themselves, they rob themselves of the freedom to change,
circling back into the identity they refuse to relinquish
in a self-perpetuating cycle of expression.
They will cling to negative energies instead of shifting
them into moments of insight and understanding.

Let go of guilt and self-loathing.
These are wasted energies that bind you to what is wrong.
Here and now, forgive yourself for your mistakes
and vow to learn and grow from them.
Take every poor choice in your life and shift it into a chance
to thrive in the future by embracing forgiveness.

You will find freedom when you choose to see
that your mistakes do not define you.

129

BE A FORCE FOR CHANGE

Be a force for positive change
by being generous with your praise and support of others.
It is a great blessing to lift another up with your words and actions.
The World is full of difficulties and everyone faces challenges.
In these times of hardship, your kindness can be a lifeline.
By taking a selfless moment to focus on the well-being of others,
you can shift the energy of an entire situation.

Many people do not feel equipped to deal with what life has thrown at them.
Your encouragement may be just what is needed
to help them break through their limitations and self-doubt.
Often, knowing that someone else cares is enough to pull a person from despair.
Become a champion of humanity and make it your business
to make the World better for everyone that you are able.
Stand for something that benefits others
and back up that stance with genuine efforts to help.

Sadly, there are many who do not care about others.
Greed, jealousy, intolerance, and personal ambitions
can lead them to damaging acts that leave lasting effects.
Make no mistake that there is evil in the World.
But do not believe you are powerless to fight it.

Be a force for change.
Start with those nearest to you and bless them
with your support and encouragement.
When you live by these ideals,
you will have stepped into a place of Spiritual awareness.
For everything is interconnected.
What harms another harms you.
What blesses another blesses you.

130

STRIP AWAY ALL FALSEHOODS

Enlightenment is commonly seen as a path,
as something that is to be gained or as a goal to be achieved.
By walking a narrow and difficult road,
it is believed that an individual will acquire clarity, peace, and joy.
However, this is not the reality of things.

Your Soul is perfect already.
It is a natural part of all of Creation.
It is already one with the Divine.
All of the blessings you could ever seek
are within your own Soul-Self right now.

Your Soul's identity is your truth.
Therefore, Enlightenment is a process
of stripping away everything that is not that truth.
It is the letting go of all that keeps you from the understanding
that you are one with Spirit,
one with all people, one with all things.

This is why most personal growth occurs
through challenges and hardships.

You are like a rock on a river bed.
Your life-situations are tumbling stones
that strike and rub against you,
removing rough edges and leaving you smoothed,
so that your surface enjoys the free-flowing water—
that is, the free-flowing Spirit of life.
Everything that is not your truth is gradually rubbed off
and removed by life's experiences.
The wise person embraces this cleansing of untruth.

This is Enlightenment.

131
FIND ENLIGHTENMENT IN LETTING GO

Do not seek Enlightenment as a goal or destination.
Instead, begin consciously to remove thoughts
and actions that lead you away
from an awareness of your interconnectedness with all existence.
Let this understanding of interconnectedness dictate your choices.
Let the awareness of your Soul's truth guide your thoughts and actions.
Let go of anything that draws you from the inner knowing of your own truth.

If you desire peace, let go of discord.
Should you seek joy, release your sorrow.
Unconditional Love can be found only where hate and condemnation are absent.
It is only by letting go of what does not reflect your Soul's identity
that Spiritual growth can occur.

Therefore, do not fight to hold on to that
which Spirit attempts to remove from you.
Let go gracefully of anything that offends your highest self.
Let go until there is nothing left within you
but the eternal light of your Soul's love.
This is the true Spirituality.
This is Enlightenment.

132
LET GO OF WORRY

Do not let your mind chase after troubles.
What might happen—as opposed to what is,
in the here and now—exists only in your thoughts.
By worrying about the future, you are harming yourself in two ways.
First, you are sending energies of fear and negativity into Creation.
This can only attract bad things, for where you place your inner focus
is where your outer experience will be.
Secondly, you are robbing yourself
of the ability to be fully present in the now.
Fears of what could happen keep a person
from experiencing the World as it is.

Why sacrifice the present moment for a future possibility?
True, what you do now will create what comes next in your life,
and it is wise to be prepared for your future.
So you should align your thoughts, words, and actions
into a cohesive energy, actively creating the life you want—
but do not do so out of fear and negative expectations or imaginings.

Be fully in the now and let that rootedness in the present
be a solid foundation on which to build your future.
Let go of exaggerated expectations and unhealthy worry,
and see yourself as capable of handling whatever may come.
Invest in your faith and know that
it will sustain you through your challenges.

Know this so fully that there is no more room
in your mind for fearful anticipations.
When you let go of worry
and bring your awareness into the present,
you free yourself to create a beautiful and happy life—
in the here and now.

133

ACT AS YOU SPEAK, SPEAK AS YOU THINK

Be direct and honest in conversation with others
and demand the same from them.
Do not make assumptions or guesses
about another's meaning and intentions.
Respect them, and yourself, enough to ask outright what they mean.
Make understanding your responsibility and seek clarity always.

Do not linger in uncertainty when
you have the power to discover real knowing.
Your Soul knows only truth as its expression.
Therefore, when you live in honesty
you are honoring your true Self.

Many people choose to be ambiguous in their conversations,
fearing to commit to an idea or stand for something strongly, out of fear of rejection.
Even more attempt to control the way others see them
by manipulating their conversations.
They project an image of what they wish to be seen as,
rather than reveal what they are in truth.
Sadly, many do not realize that their true self-identity
would have found greater and more lasting acceptance
than any distorted image ever could.

Choose your words wisely and speak only what you truly mean.
Beyond that, honor your words with matching actions,
again demanding the same of those around you.

Act as you speak.
Speak as you think.

This is integrity.

1334

EMBRACE CHANGE

You must create room for what you want in your life.
Most people's lives are so full that they have no space for new experiences.
They keep themselves from having what they want
by holding too tightly to what they already have.
They cling to the familiar, even when it no longer serves them.
They will speak often of what they desire
while holding on to things that no longer bring them the joy they once did
and in no way match what they wish to create in life.

Insecurity, doubt, and fear of the unknown
will keep some trapped in their current situations.
Sentimentality and thoughts of what once were will ensnare others,
even when it is no longer the truth of the situation.
Your every circumstance and connection have value.
This is certain, as they could not have come into your life if this were not true.
But, just as situations change in life as you grow and evolve in your truth,
so will your connections to other people.
Circumstances and individuals will come into your life
for a reason and may leave your life when that reason is satisfied.
The blessing comes through letting go.

It is a moment of honoring the newness of your expression,
and of theirs, by releasing the old.
Respect yourself and those who share time with you
by accepting end points without resistance or regret.
Sadly, many will refuse to let go with one hand
until they have something firmly grasped in the other.
This is not faith.
This is not trust.

Be cautious during times of change,
but not to the point of being frozen in inaction.
Embrace change.
Learn to let go.

135
PRACTICE GRATITUDE

Take moments throughout your day to practice gratitude
and acceptance, regardless of your present circumstances.
In doing this, you will grant yourself peace of mind,
even when you want things to be different.

Far too many people treat contentment and happiness
as outcomes rather than as attitudes.
They will suffer whenever things do not turn out as they would prefer.
Their efforts will become meaningless to them,
because the outcomes differ from their expectations.
The negativity associated with seeming failures
will only create more obstacles and problems.

As discontentment grows, happiness becomes an elusive prospect
that can only be acquired through attaining the next goal.
As this cycle of negativity feeds on itself,
disappointment becomes part of one's identity.

Break free from such energies by focusing on gratitude.
Even when an outcome differs from one's intention, there is much to be celebrated.
Find gratitude for the inspiration that led you to set goals:
applaud yourself for trying.

Be thankful that you have a life to change:
this alone is reason to be joyous.

Open yourself to the understanding that happiness
and contentment are choices
independent of one's circumstances and achievements.

Choose today to be happiness
instead of chasing it.

136
AFFIRM OTHER PEOPLE'S CHOICES

Do not overly involve or concern yourself
with the affairs of others.
Allow their journeys to be their own.
What you would do in a situation
in no way dictates what another person should do.
The happiest people in life learn to not attach themselves
to the choices and actions of others.
They focus on their own issues with a clear sense of priorities.

Learn the difference between helping when asked and meddling when not.
Many of the evils of the World are simply not yours to fix.

Many people waste time and energy worrying about situations
that have no direct effect on their lives
while ignoring larger issues that truly matter.
Some will take a healthy sense of caring
and exaggerate it in ways that make a situation
seem about them personally.
They will attach themselves to whatever drama is going on around them,
just to be involved.

This need to control another's circumstances and choices
may reflect a lack of feeling in control of one's own life.
Avoid this negativity by focusing on your own affairs.

Set boundaries about your own life and choose wisely
where you involve yourself with others.
Learn to accept that others are free to act
and respond to life as they will.
Celebrate individuality and freedom of choice
in everyone you meet.

137

ASK WHAT YOU ARE HERE TO LEARN

There will be times when you feel you have no answers
and no idea of what you should do.
It is completely understandable to admit times of doubt,
of desperation, of feeling weak or lost.
However, you can never truly be lost.

You are a child of Spirit and, no matter what is going on in your life,
you are exactly where you need to be.
Though the reasons may seem unclear and the next step elusive,
know that every moment is a blessing.
Every circumstance is a chance to dig deeper into your faith,
into yourself, and redefine your responses to the World.

Everything you experience is there to give you a greater understanding of your own Self.
Instead of understanding the situation merely, make self-understanding your goal.

When you find yourself lacking clarity and you don't know what to do, go within.
Take some quiet time and connect with Divinity.
Let go of the problem and let your mind rest in confidence that everything is as it should be.
Believe that you have been led to this point, no matter what is going on, by Spirit.
Become calm and certain that the answers you seek will present themselves.
Take the fear of unknowing away and replace it with faith.

Open your mind to ask what lessons you are meant to learn.
The direction you should take will be shown to you.

Live with the knowing that you have always been led
and will always find yourself right where you need to be
for your Soul to grow and flourish.
When you look at your life from a Soul perspective,
every moment is a blessing, every situation a chance to learn,
and every choice an opportunity
to re-create the Self.

138

BE BOLD IN LIVING YOUR TRUTH

Cast away suffering and embrace celebration.
What makes you different is what makes you incredible.
The very nature of the Universe is one of creation and expression.
The seemingly limitless variety of life in the natural World illustrates this boldly.
It is full of color and sound, uniqueness and difference.
You do not question the blessing of this diversity and should not question your own.
You are equally Divine.

Every great accomplishment in human history was born out of
someone who had the willingness to stand apart and do things differently
than it had been done before.
The greatest artists, inventors, and entertainers have embraced their individuality
and shared it with the World.
In order for you to find real happiness in this life, you must do two things.

First, you must discover your truth.
Go within yourself and find what makes you special.
Uncover your gift.
Second, you must share what you have discovered with the World.
Choose to make truth, rather than approval or acceptance, your motivator.
Know that when you embrace your own truth,
those who do not appreciate you will fall away
and new people will be magnetized to you.
They will validate you,
because they know the value of being true to Self.

Set aside fear.
Be bold in living your truth.
Find a way to share yourself openly.
In this way you honor your Soul
and bless the World
with your light.

139

AVOID JEALOUSY

Jealousy is a poison that destroys some relationships
and keeps others from forming.
Even when it is unspoken, jealousy siphons away joy.

The inability to be happy for another person is damaging
both to the person envied and to the one holding resentment.
When you hold envy in your heart,
you rob the other person of the freedom to enjoy success
and the energy that comes with it.

Some will even sabotage the accomplishments of others
because they cannot stand for others to have what they lack.
Through their insecurity, they will find it impossible
to enjoy the successes of others.

When you are jealous of another, you are sending a belief out into the Universe
that there is not enough of whatever you seek to go around.
It is a mindset of lack that will only manifest itself
as further emptiness in your life.

Avoid this by finding sincere happiness
for everyone who obtains their desires.
Know, beyond any doubt, that the Universe is
a place of limitless abundance for everyone.
Congratulate others for their accomplishments
and you will create an energy of success
for your own life.

140

BE ACTIVE IN YOUR SPIRITUALITY

It is not enough to have beliefs and convictions.
You must live them outwardly.

Far too many people claim beliefs that they never actually live.
They will set words in place of actions and live their lives by a double standard.
Many of these same people will condemn others for not believing as they do.
They will spend their time in judgment
rather than working to uplift others
or even dealing with their own shortcomings.

This is a self-serving mindset that does not reflect the truth of Spirit.
All the great prophets and teachers have spoken and lived by the same ideals.
As they have shown, to live in Spirit is to practice love,
compassion, acceptance, and service to others.
These are actions that, when lived fully,
will take you deeper into your connection with the Divine
than any muttered words or self-righteous condemnations.

Stop telling people how spiritual you are and show them.
Speak of love most often as an account of your actions toward others.
Learn the difference between having beliefs and living them.

Choose to be an example of compassion and service,
and in doing so, inspire others to action in the name of Spirit.
In this way you can not only live your spiritual truth,
but also make the World a better place for everyone.
This is what it means
to be alive in faith.

Do not spend your time regretting the loss of what once was.
When it is time for something to fade from your life, let it go gracefully.
Accept and acknowledge the good that came from the situation
and hold tightly to that part; at the same time,
trust that, by letting go, you are creating space in your World
for something new and amazing.

Far too many people cling to outdated situations
and to connections with people who no longer fit their lives.
They will allow sentimentality and familiarity to keep them from moving forward.
Many hold on to the possibility that the other person can change—
which blinds them to truth of that other person's expression.
Sadly, some fall victim to abusive behavior because of this.

Value yourself enough to let go of those who do not uplift you.
By releasing negative people—even those you once held dear—
from your life, you create an opportunity to redefine yourself.

To find the blessing that comes with letting go, look at a flower.
When the seed falls and the flower begins to fade,
the seed does not mourn the loss of what once was.
Instead, it takes root and grows into its own beautiful expression.
In this same way you can find beauty in your own life.

Do not become a hoarder of people, slowly suffocated
by those who should long since have faded away.
Decide today to share your life only with those who love and support you.
Give yourself permission to let go of what is not right in your life and,
in doing so, grow and thrive
as you were meant to all along.

142

CHOOSE HAPPINESS

The happiest people are those who understand
that, rather than circumstance,
choice and attitude determine their experience of any given situation.
They choose their responses rather than give into reaction.
They do not allow externals to steal their peace of mind.

People who approach life in this way change the situations around them,
rather than the situations' changing them.
They realize that everything in this World is temporary,
so they strive to find the best in each moment.
The wise learn to let go of what they cannot control,
affect for the better everything they can,
and choose to be happy either way.

Others, unfortunately, adopt sadness as their way of being
and see every moment through this dark attitude.
Their attitude sucks the joy out of the present moment,
both for themselves and for everyone around them.

The way you approach life is the way life will approach you.
This is the law of Creation.
Choose happiness.

Decide today that you alone will determine your attitude
and make it one of expecting greatness.
Do everything you can to make the life you want
and know that, regardless of what happens,
your happiness is a choice that only you can make.
Make that decision here and now.
Smile with your entire being.

143

TREAT OTHERS AS YOU WOULD BE TREATED

Make kindness both your action and your expectation.
When you act out of love and compassion, you are elevating yourself
and the other person as well.
For those on the Spiritual path this begins to come easily,
as love and compassion are inherent qualities of the Soul.
Such people understand that everyone is connected in Spirit;
hence, to act negatively toward another is to act negatively toward the self.

What you send into this World will most certainly return to you.
For those who understand this, the ideas of acceptance
and charity become first nature;
they will bless people everywhere they go.
Unfortunately, many of these same individuals
will not place an equal demand upon how they are treated.
They will allow their own self-loathing to distort their actions,
tainting these with darkness.

Do not stand for such behaviors in your life.
Be loving, be kind, and demand the same from those around you.
Set boundaries in your interactions and be prepared to dismiss
from your life those who choose not to respect them.
Honor the boundaries of others in this same way.

When you set an example led by Spirit,
it will be one of love and kindness.

144
HEAL YOURSELF BY HELPING OTHERS

If you wish to know how to help others,
go within and find your own pain.
Discover where you suffer and why.
Ask yourself the hard questions and don't run from your truth.
Then seek out those who hurt in the same way
that you do and help them.

Trust that Spirit has gifted you with personal experiences, for good and for ill,
that have given you the awareness to help someone else.
You will understand their fears and limitations.
You will be able to give comfort where others could not.
Your words of encouragement will come from a place of knowing.

Be the support for someone else that you wish you had had for yourself.
It is natural to want to avoid things that remind you of your pain.
It is equally natural to want to avoid the pain still dwelling inside.
Neither avoidance serves your growth.

By stepping into service to others in areas that troubled you,
you begin to alter the experience—
both for yourself and for the person you strive to help.

You will change your focus to resolutions rather than repetitions.
Your energies will shift into a place of healing rather than hurting.
You will also discover the amazing truth that elevating others
is the greatest gift you can give yourself.

Choose today to turn your experience, no matter how painful,
into a blessing for someone else.
In this way you will find
freedom and blessings.

145

LET YOUR ACTIONS SPEAK FOR YOU

What you do defines you much more than what you say.
Far too many people talk endlessly about what they are going to do:
they will speak of their convictions and beliefs,
their goals and intentions, but never take those thoughts into action.
Having the right mindset is crucial for growth and success in life—
but this is only true when it is backed up by action.

When you set an intention,
you have aligned yourself energetically with what you seek.
What you believe and expect will create opportunities for you
to experience what you desire;
but opportunities are not the experience itself.
It is only when you find the motivation to act on opportunities that
you will reap the rewards of what you have created.

When you fall into the habit of saying one thing
and doing another, or doing nothing at all,
you will lose the respect and support of those around you.
People will begin to expect words instead of actions
and their belief in you will fade.

Become the master of your own life:
embrace integrity by doing what you say and your World
will reward you with new experiences, new joys.
You will become known as a person of action
and gain great respect and validation.
When you choose to make your actions match your words,
you will be living in truth.
Happiness is sure to follow.

146

LET FAITH SUSTAIN YOU

Every dark moment in your life
is meant to remind you of the light you carry within.
Every challenge you face is a reminder that,
through faith and perseverance, you can weather life's storms.
Do not doubt for one moment that you are capable of making it
through any situation that confronts you.
Know you were meant to thrive and that every seeming obstacle
is really a chance to realign yourself with what you desire
by shifting your approach.

Develop a strong sense of faith to sustain you in hard times.
There will be times when you feel that you lack the inspiration
or energy to respond to life's demands.
The challenges will seem too many and the answers too few.
You will question your actions and doubt your choices.
You may find yourself wanting to give up.

Even in these moments, carry yourself with the conviction
and nobility of one who is born from Spirit.
Trust that the part of you that is connected to the Divine
will sustain you, even during your darkest trials.

Remember that you are not defined by your problems.
You are defined by your responses to them.
When you stand in your faith and set your will to the task of moving forward,
you will begin to shift the energies of the situation toward resolution.
Your determination, coupled with your faith in Spirit,
will help you rise above what might otherwise drag you down.

Trust yourself and, beyond that, trust Spirit.
The light you carry within you, that Divine spark that is your Soul,
is bright beyond your imaginings and can illuminate
even the darkest corners of your life.

Many people surrender to obstacles or delays,
letting go of what they desire because
it isn't easy or instantly grasped.
They will begin things with no real commitment or follow-through.
Some will even blame Spirit, claiming that things
that do not come easily were not meant to be.

In truth, this surrendering often results from feelings
of self-doubt or of being undeserving.
You cannot hope to have what you want in this life
if you do not believe you deserve it
or are unwilling to put forth the effort.
Perseverance is the key to attaining your goals.

The most successful people are relentless
in their pursuit of what they desire.
They see each roadblock as an opportunity
to reevaluate their approach but not as a stopping point.
They will devote real time in real actions
rather than merely speaking about what could be.
They will apply themselves in every capacity,
never believing that their goals will be unmet.
It is this certainty that will lead them to accomplishment.

Take ownership and responsibility for your life and your happiness.
Set goals and intentions, knowing you deserve good things.
Give genuine effort and perseverance toward what you want.
Be a constant force of change and betterment in your own life.

When you live in this way, the World becomes a place of opportunities
and accomplishments
for you to enjoy.

148
LOVE YOURSELF IN SOUL AND BODY

Your body is a sacred temple
in which your Soul resides.
It is the vessel your highest Self has chosen and it is the one thing
you will carry with you until you step back into Spirit.
It should be revered and cherished, cared for and loved.
To accept yourself means to embrace not only the parts you like,
but also the aspects you would wish to change.
Embrace your higher thinking and emotions,
but also live with ownership and acceptance of the body.

This cannot be.
Everything in existence is ultimately a part of Divinity.
Every flower, mountain, and tree is a part of Spirit.
The stars, the rivers, and the winds are all part of a magnificent beauty
that is the expression of the Divine.
Every single thing in existence is a thread in a great tapestry.
How then could your entire self not also be connected in this same way?

Even if you seek to change your physical form,
begin by claiming and accepting it in the here and now.
Love your body and see it as just as much a part of your truth as your Soul.
Work as diligently on your physical state as you do on your mental and emotional selves.
Just as you should not take in negative thoughts and opinions from others,
be equally mindful of the foods you eat and the activities you engage in.
Train the mind and emotions to find focus and clarity,
but remember also to train the body to keep it strong and healthy.
When you want changes in your life,
approach them with the wholeness
of your being.

Own every part of yourself.

149
CELEBRATE OTHERS' DIFFERENCES

One key to happiness
is to realize that others have differing attitudes
and opinions and that you neither have to agree with them
nor change your thinking because theirs do not match your own.
A great freedom comes when you accept the differences among human beings.
When you step away from the need for approval and stand firmly in your truth,
you will have accomplished a greatly rewarding task.

There will be occasions when someone will offer you timely and needed advice—
advice that will help you along in your journey or in understanding life's challenges.
These moments will resonate deeply within you and should be valued greatly.
You will recognize these instances by the selfless and supportive energy
held by the one offering advice.

However, the criticisms and judgments of others
will most often stem from their own experiences.
They will tell you quite emphatically how you should think
and act and even how you should feel.
Their mandates will be more a reflection of where they are in life than where you are.
Rarely will they be in your best interest, free from the other person's agenda.

Even when manipulation isn't the motive,
the other person cannot fully understand the road you have traveled
or the reasons for your choices.
Let go of needing them to.

Honor your individual expression and
extend that respect to the choices of others,
even when they do not match your own.
In doing so, you will free your Soul to express itself fully.
What greater happiness could there be?

150
CREATE YOUR OWN IDENTITY

Do not let your burdens define you or identify you.
You are far more than a collection of problems.
Dwelling on what is not right in your World
only invites sadness and adds energy to the problem.
That energy would be better used toward resolutions.

Unfortunately, many will choose to allow their circumstances to define them,
rather than allow their inner convictions to direct their response to life.
You will either live your life with the understanding
that you are free to create your own identity,
or you will allow life to choose one for you.

You must understand that life is not something that is happening to you.
You have to let go of the idea that everything is either a reward or a punishment.
The way you approach life is the way life will approach you.
Step away from feeling that some are blessed and some are not.
This is not the way of things.

Your life is not a cruel game.
It is a series of events and circumstances that
you are free to respond to as you feel is best.
Choose those responses wisely and with the full knowledge
that you are meant to thrive and be happy.
Replace the identity of being one who carries burdens
with one of being blessed and empowered.
Do this regardless of what is happening in any given moment
and your life will shift, changing for the better.
See yourself as a child of the Divine, blessed by your very nature—
and your life will become
joyous and free.

151

CHALLENGE YOURSELF

How can you hope to grow if you do not challenge yourself?
How can you thrive when you choose to revisit old, limiting patterns and habits?
New and exciting experiences await you when you let go
of your old identities for the sake of creating new ones.

One of the greatest steps toward happiness
is to let go of the old self when that identity no longer serves you,
even when you are uncertain of your new way of being.
You can never really understand this new Self until you step fully into it.
Cast off all self-limitations.

Realize that you are capable of more
than you have allowed yourself to believe.
No one is good at everything, but everyone is good at something.
Seek out your truth.
Challenge yourself!

Begin by recognizing the areas where you are stuck,
and decide today to break out of those patterns.
Make yourself uncomfortable for the best of reasons: personal growth.
Let go of habits, thoughts, and even people that hold you down.
Try new things, even when the prospect scares you.

When you decide to challenge yourself
to grow and take those thoughts into action,
you will generate an energy of change
that will ripple out into your entire World,
filling it with wonder
and excitement.

152
SEEK EMPOWERMENT

Choose to define yourself,
or situations and people around you will do it for you.
Individuals have free will and the right to express their truth.
However, many people allow their identities to be dictated and shaped
by the demands and expectations of others.
Some will allow a particular circumstance to define them,
clinging to an identity that was thrust upon them
by external pressures rather than
standing strongly in their inner convictions.
Insecurity, lack of acceptance, and fear
will force some people to take on thoughts and actions
that are not really of their choosing.
Many times they will say something
other than what they truly feel,
just to avoid confrontation.
Sadly, some will even use the expectations of others as an excuse,
blaming them for their own shortcomings or lack of efforts.

These are not fitting approaches to life for
one seeking empowerment and happiness.
You were born from Spirit and given a most
precious possession—your free will.
You came to this place to find your individual expression and to set it free.

None of this is to say that you shouldn't do for others
or take them into consideration.
It is, however, a call to seek out those individuals who revel
in your uniqueness and celebrate your expression.
When you share your truth with others,
you are giving both them and yourself an amazing gift.
Take quiet time away from others and, in those moments,
seek your own truth, your definition.
Then find every way you possibly can to live within that truth.

In this way you empower yourself and your Spirit
will shine through you for all to see.

153

RELAX AND LET GO

Do not become so busy with the labors of life
or so burdened by its challenges that you lose sight
of the beauty and wonder all around you.
So many people rush from one activity to the next so quickly
that they cannot enjoy the moment.

No matter your ambitions or problems,
take time to breathe and enjoy the inherent beauty
that is all around you in the natural World.
The World is filled with so many great and amazing things
that you do not have to look far to realize the perfection of Spirit.
Allow the accomplishments of others to inspire you
to live your own fullest potential.
See their kindnesses as a reminder to live this way yourself.
Let laughter remind you to not take yourself so seriously.
Revel in the uniqueness of Spirit
that is shown through every person you meet.
Realize that you too are part of these Divine expressions
and that you too are unique and beautiful
in your own right.

Yes, you came here to learn.
But, in truth, there is only one lesson.
It is to remember that you are a Soul within a body
and that you are ultimately part of Divinity.
You are only passing through this place.
Choose today to enjoy the journey.
Relax and let go.

See the beauty and wonder of this World
as but a reflection of the grandeur within your own self
and your life will become filled
with joy and amazement.

1544

SPEAK AS IF IN PRAYER

Be mindful of your words,
for they have incredible power.
They are thoughts and intentions placed upon the breath,
which holds the life-force energy.
The good or bad you choose to place upon those words
will have a very real impact on your personal experiences
and on those who hear them.

When you speak negatively about yourself,
you diminish your own vibration.
You lessen yourself and your potentials.
When you fall into excessive complaining about your life,
you are only adding energy to the negative experience
and reinforcing what is wrong.
This hurtful self-dialogue has a very real and lasting impact upon your life.
Likewise, when you choose to use your words negatively toward others,
you are directing malicious and harmful energies at them.

These energies will return to you, for this is the law of the Universe.
The hurt that can be inflicted by harmful words is immeasurable.
It can change the very course of a person's life.

Do not fool yourself into believing that your words have no impact.
This is simply an excuse to be reckless in speech
and to avoid responsibility for what you put forth.
Your words can do real harm.
Or they can do real good.

Speak every word as if
it were part of a prayer.

155

SPEAK THROUGH LOVE

There is a blessing that is available to you,
and everyone you meet, through the choice of right speaking.
Begin with your inner dialogue.
Adjust what you say to yourself internally:
move from negativity and criticism to validation and acceptance.

Let love become your inner voice.
Make what you say to yourself uplifting and inspiring, encouraging and happy.
Then let these attitudes become your voice in the World.
Begin to speak aloud your good intentions and beliefs
that you are able to achieve greatness.
Decide today to spend much more time talking
about what is right in your life than what is wrong.
Help and heal your own life in this way.

Be conscious and in control of every word and you will begin
to master your own experiences in life.
You will also enrich the lives of others
when you extend this way of talking to them.

Be kind in your words.
Be truthful and generous when you speak to others.
Let your words be the voice of Spirit coming through you
and you will bless your own life
and the lives of all
who hear you.

156

BE SELF-CENTERED, NOT SELFISH

Establish firmly within yourself the difference between
being selfish and being Self-centered.
Selfish people will think only of themselves.
All of their choices and actions will be based on what serves them best
with no regard to how they might affect others.
They will often be led by greed and a need for power over others.
Although they will readily accept the help and kindness offered by other people,
they will only extend these same energies to others
when they feel it will ultimately benefit them to do so.
The selfish person only knows taking and blaming,
never owning their responsibilities.
They will live with a fear that if they do not take from others—
be it material possessions,
time or emotions—they will not have enough.

This type of thinking stems from a belief
that there is only so much abundance
and happiness to go around.
This simply is not true.

Self-centered people, however,
approach life in a very different way.
They understand that all people share in the common reality of life,
though their individual experience within that reality
emanates from deep within themselves.
They will own their present situations as result of their actions.
They live life as an opportunity to create with a full understanding
that what they create comes from within,
even as it radiates out into the World and affects others.
They will live life with the understanding
that they are truly the centers of their own Universes,
and that everyone else is the center
of his or her own Universe, as well.

157

REMEMBER YOUR SOUL-SELF

It is normal for you to doubt yourself at times,
especially when it is hard to see where your path is leading.
Life's challenges will sometimes seem quite overwhelming,
and everyone has moments
when they feel inadequate
to the challenges they face.

There will be times you will want to give up,
believing that your situation is bigger than you.
However, the truth is that you are uniquely qualified
to deal with whatever obstacle you face.
Your higher Self aligned you with it, because it is what you need to grow.
The problem, your response to it, and its solution all emanate from within you.
Every experience you have is meant to lead you back to faith.

Everything that you encounter, good or bad,
is to remind you that you are a Soul
and that you are just passing through this place
on your way back home.
When you invest in a true sense of this understanding,
you will begin to see all things as temporary.
Moments will come and they will pass.
This is not what is important.
Your response to them is.

Remind yourself often that your trials are temporary
and that they will pass;
you can move through them with faith and confidence.
Replace doubt with faith and fear with a knowing that all is as it should be.
Allow each experience to remind you
that there is something greater than this worldly life
and that your Soul is a part of it.

158

BE GENEROUS

The key to prosperity in all things
is to be generous in all things.
When you let go of belief in lack and limitation,
you are freed to give and receive.
The Universe is a place of abundance
and the creative force of Spirit is limitless.

It is only the belief in limitation
that keeps people from experiencing the joy that comes from living these truths.
Many people become miserly with their affections, interactions, and of course, money.
They will hoard their possessions and emotions,
fearful that if they share those parts of themselves
they will fall into lack.

What you put forth into the World
will reflect back to you.
This is an absolute truth.
If you want love, give love.
When you need comfort, seek opportunities
to offer it to someone who is hurting.

Be generous with your time and attention.
Stand ready to be in service to others in whatever way you can.
Believe that there is more than enough goodness for all.
Whether it is time, money, or simply a kind word, be generous.
Be as giving as you are able.

When you make this your true way of being,
the Universe will open up to you.
The key to living a blessed life
is to be a blessing to others.

159
LOVE YOURSELF UNCONDITIONALLY

Love is one of the most powerful
and transformative forces in the Universe.
It has the power to change everything it touches.
It is limitless in its ability to heal, uplift, and bless.
Love binds people together.
It is selfless.
It is the very essence of Spirit and is a part of every Soul in existence.
Love is abundantly available to everyone.

Why then do so many seek love and never seem to find it?
How can something this abundant and ever present be so elusive to so many?
The answer is that people fail to love themselves first.

When you deny yourself of a sense of inner love,
it becomes impossible to feel love from others.
Many people deny themselves the joy of experiencing love
from other people because they devalue themselves.
They will judge some aspect of themselves unworthy because of some perceived flaw.
They will confuse something they do not like about themselves
with the belief that they are unlovable.
This cannot be true.

All beings are born from, and deserving of, love.
Go within yourself and discover why you do not feel self-love.
Isolate the reasons you refuse love and acceptance for yourself.
Resolve or rise above whatever you find.
Give yourself permission to love yourself fully here and now.

Let your love be absolute
and without conditions.

160

GIVE LOVE FREELY AND WITHOUT EXPECTATION

Do not confuse personal boundaries with limiting love.
You have the right and responsibility
to choose the people you interact with.
However, this should not lead you to withhold love
unless your personal criteria are met.
Do not allow love to become something
that is bought by words or interactions.
Love is not meant to be a reward given only to those
who act as you would have them.
Allow it to stand as an absolute,
unwavering and powerful.

Some will seem unworthy of your love.
Be loving anyway.
In truth, those seeming to deserve love the least need it the most.
Decide that loving is your natural state of being.

Give love freely and without expectation.
When you act out of love, all of your actions
become part of a dance of Spirit that blesses all of Creation.
When you find love for yourself and choose to send that love into the World,
it will assuredly reflect back to you.

What you seek in life you must first find within yourself.
Understand this truth and you will find the path
to love in all areas of your life.

161
FEEL THE PRESENCE OF LOST LOVED ONES

Though you will mourn the loss of those you love,
you should also celebrate their Souls' freedom.
When people pass from this World,
it is because this particular part of their Souls' journeys are completed.
They have experienced and learned what they came here for and have returned home.
Their burdens and suffering have ended
and they are now freed into their true identities
as bright, shining Spirits.

Their physical beings may fade
but this does not mean they are lost to you.
Their energy is a part of you and they will travel with you
until you are able to join them on the other side.
You will see their faces everywhere.
Their voices will be ever present in your mind
and their words will fall from the mouths of those around you.
Their presences will surround you and manifest at every possible opportunity.

By acknowledging these moments,
you will strengthen the new connection you now share with them.
Open yourself to the idea that your relationship
to those who have passed may have changed but that it is not gone.
Speak to them often and then listen for their responses.
Trust that the feelings of their beings around you
are real and validate their presences.

In this way you honor the dead and increase your awareness
that everyone in existence is a glorious Soul
within a physical body and that, in truth,
all are eternal.

162
SEE LOSS AS CHANGE

When you mourn the passing of a loved one
by acknowledging the limitlessness of their Spirit,
you remind yourself that you too are limitless in your abilities and potentials.
Regardless of the circumstances of their passing,
know that they will find comfort and peace in Spirit.
Allow yourself to let go of thoughts
that something could have been different
or that you should have done more.
Trust that all is just as it should be.

Let sorrow give way to new experiences, new interactions.
Do not speak in terms of loss, but rather of change, of transition.
This is a more accurate reflection of the truth.

Know that every person passes through this World
but is not truly of this World:
This knowledge brings freedom and acceptance.

Mourn the loss of the physical but not of the Spirit.
Those you love are never truly lost to you.
When you think of them, let it bring a smile rather than tears.
Let the love you have for those you care about reach beyond the grave
and strive to keep them as an active part of your life.
This is true memorial.

This is the greatest blessing
you can give them and yourself.

163
AVOID COMPLACENCY

Learn to listen to yourself and put what you discover within into action.
Trust that you, more than anyone else, know what is best for your life.
Give yourself permission here and now to be the authority in your World.
This is your birthright and the truth of your existence.

Many people give up their free will too easily.
They will doubt themselves and, in doing so,
will allow others to make choices for them.
In self-doubt, they will believe they are incapable
of making right decisions and refuse to take action.
Their lives will begin to revolve around the desires
of others rather than their own ambitions.

Do not fall into this trap of personal complacency and laziness.
Stop settling for life as it presents itself or as others would have you live it.
Instead, become a force for personal change and betterment.

Quit making excuses for not living the life you imagine.
Take action toward what you desire
rather than waiting for whatever comes next in life.
Ask yourself often what would make you happy
and give your attention and efforts
toward whatever that may be.

Quit limiting your own experiences through lack of effort.
Realize that you deserve happiness as much as anyone else
and that it is your responsibility to create it.

Become relentless in your personal pursuits
and make your own happiness your greatest focus.
When you do this you will be adding joy to this World,
and in that way you will benefit
all of humanity.

1644

CHOOSE YOUR PATH

The path you walk in life will be of your own making.
It is up to you to set your intentions and strive
to become the person you envision yourself to be.
Happiness comes to those who reach for their own potentials
and are willing to cast off old identities and ways of being.
Such people embrace their newfound selves.

There can be many challenges along the way.
However, to find yourself and your joy
is one of the greatest things you will ever do.
Sometimes it is difficult to move forward in life,
because it means leaving people that you love behind.
Many limit themselves by clinging to the familiar.
They allow their feelings for others to dictate or limit their actions.
They will choose not to pursue what they know would fulfill them
out of a sense of loyalty or affection,
fearing they will not be loved if they change.

Sadly, some people in your life will withhold their love
unless you act in accordance with their expectations.
This is not love.

Love is acceptance.
Love is celebration of individuality.
Love is validation.
It is a freedom, not a limitation.

165

HONOR EACH PERSON'S CHOICES

When those in your life
choose not to move forward with you,
you are given a choice.
You can allow their limitations to become your own;
or, you can honor the individuality of personal expression in all of its forms.
You should neither demand that they change with you
nor stop your own evolution.

Those who will bless your journey
do not need be coerced into doing so.
Those who walk freely alongside you
are the ones deserving of your time and attention.

Let your connections to others change as you yourself change.
Welcome all you love to journey through life with you,
and bless them when they choose a different path.
The wise understand that,
although the roads taken in life may be different,
they all lead to the same place.
Each separate path ultimately leads every Soul back home,
back to the great Oneness.

Be comforted by this when you are faced with letting go
of someone you care about for the sake of your own growth.
Honor each person's choices.
Do this first with yourself:
you will find that your path
becomes lighter and more joyous as
you follow the direction of your own Soul
rather than the expectations of others.

166
LET GO OF SELF-CRITICISM

Strive for excellence in all things,
but do not confuse excellence with perfection.
You will make mistakes.
You will stumble upon your own path,
sometimes wondering if there is a path for you to follow at all.
You may find yourself envying others who seem to have
"figured out" life or enjoy some success that you desire for yourself.
Do not allow yourself to be troubled by such things.

The life you envy is filled with its own difficulties.
You cannot possibly understand the life of another.
It is too easy to presume things about other people
and to place them above yourself in your perceptions.
Even more than falsely elevating others,
you must avoid diminishing yourself.
Realize that you are in competition with no one.

Make it your goal to understand yourself better
and learn from your experiences,
but to do so without self-condemnation.
Decide today to forgive yourself for any shortcomings
and rise into an awareness that you are
as deserving of happiness as anyone else on this Earth.

Let go of self-criticism and the sense of failure.
Quit comparing lives.
Replace perfection with personal excellence
and focus more on the moment: value your efforts as much as the outcomes.
Find appreciation for what you learn about yourself
through your mistakes and grow from that self-understanding.

Step into the knowledge that you are a timeless Soul
and that you are excellent in your own fashion.
Own this knowledge and you will
also own happiness.

167
CHOOSE HAPPINESS

Your happiness matters.
It is yours to seize at any opportunity.
You alone know best what would make you happy.
If you do not know your happiness,
then you must begin by delving deeply
into your inner Self to find the answer.
This is difficult for many,
because they are not accustomed to such Soul questions.

Life contains a great many challenges, but also opportunities for great joy.
Where you place your focus and your willingness to act
on your desires will dictate which is more prevalent in your life.

Be ambitious when it comes to your happiness.
Decide that the perfect time for change in your life is now.
Set goals and work toward them.

Claim your right to joyfulness and work tirelessly toward it.
Being in service to others always brings happiness
and should be a part of your life,
but make time for your personal pleasure as well.

Cast aside the guilt many feel
when they serve themselves.
Save for the truly selfish-minded,
this guilt is unnecessary and harmful.

The time for action is now.
Be happiness in thought,
word, and deed.

168
FIND HAPPINESS WITHIN

Most people look for happiness in the wrong places.
They are convinced that satisfaction lies outside of themselves.
They will fill their lives with material things,
but this will only bring temporary satisfaction.
They will mimic others for the sake of acceptance
and lose themselves in the process.
They will look for answers through other people,
yet their truest guidance already rests within them.

Yes, there are many wondrous things to be experienced outwardly in this life,
and the answers to your questions will present themselves
at every available point in your World.
However, neither the joy of life's pleasures
nor the messages from Spirit
will ever matter if you do not see them
as radiating from the core of your being.

Your ability to connect outwardly
depends on your ability to connect inwardly.
You must find an inner stillness to discover
the magnificence of Creation that resides within you.
Begin to see everything you experience
as a reflection of your inner sacred space
and you will be led to greatness in your life.

Trust yourself and go within.
When you do this, all of your questions will find answers
and your life will be filled with the happiness
that comes from living
as a Divine being.

169
STRIVE FOR SIMPLICITY

Many people overcomplicate their lives.
Their frantic and reckless race for success
and accomplishment keeps them dissatisfied with life.
Feeling that they are not doing enough with their lives,
they fill the void with whatever comes along.
They invest time and energy in things that don't truly matter.
Their drive to achieve what society values
robs them of the joy of following their own hearts' desires.
Their thoughts of what might happen have no basis in reality,
and yet they allow fear to dictate actions.
Some cling to complications, whether real or imagined,
to excuse themselves from taking action to better their lives.

Choose simplicity instead.
Allow obvious answers to satisfy you.
Unravel the entanglements you have created in your life
and free yourself to pursue what would really make you happy.

When recounting your challenges to others, do not give in to exaggeration.
Allow yourself to be bigger than your circumstances in your own mind,
and you will become empowered to change them.
Become uncomplicated in your approach to your life
and your life will itself become
uncomplicated and joyous.

170
RECOGNIZE YOUR TRUE VALUE

Your self-worth can be determined
by how fully you accept yourself.
It cannot be measured by money or possessions.
It lies not in the way others see you
or in their opinions of the way you live your life.
It isn't even found in your accomplishments.

Your true value is found in the recognition
that you are a Soul, connected to all
other Souls, all other things, and that because of this you are amazing.
You are perfect in your imperfections,
and it is only your ability to accept and love yourself
that determines your self-worth.

People will judge you, but this is not your worth.
You may fall into comparisons with others, but this is not your worth.
These are merely distorted reflections and opinions.
The moment you place your value in the hands of another, you are lost.
Do not give yourself away so easily.

Regardless of your perceived flaws you are magnificent.
Love and value yourself even when no one else seems to.
Let go of false ideas of perfection.
Strive always for betterment, but do not let this steal
your sense of value in the here and now.
Love yourself, all of yourself, and you will begin to understand
true self-worth and the freedom
that comes with it.

171
TEND YOUR INNER GARDEN

Negativity is a weed that grows
in the peaceful garden of the mind.
If not removed, it will choke out the positive thoughts,
expectations, and beliefs that lead to happiness.
Negativity has a way of corrupting one's perspective.
It can shift one's entire energy and, therefore, one's experiences in life.

How you see your World internally is how you will experience it externally.
Complaining only feeds the cycle of negative growth within your thoughts.
When you fall into complaint rather than striving for resolution,
you have given power to what is wrong in your life.
Every time you speak of how great your challenges are,
they will grow in their power over you.

You must decide
the energies with which you want to align yourself.
Only you can make this choice.
It is solely your responsibility to weed out of your thoughts
that which does not serve your highest good.
Take direct action toward remedies to problems,
and rise above what you cannot change through acceptance.

Tend your garden with positive words, intentions, and expectations.
Choose to become the master gardener of your thoughts.
Tend those thoughts with positive words and actions.

By doing so, your inner garden will flourish,
and beauty will radiate from within
to fill your World with joy.

172
PURSUE YOUR PASSIONS

What are you passionate about?
What excites and thrills you?
What motivates you?
These questions should be easily answered,
yet some people are unable to do so.
They will have let go of their dreams and aspirations,
often having never attempted them.
Many will allow conformity and the need for acceptance
to rob passion from their lives.
They will work jobs they do not care about or even like.
They may lose their individuality by mimicking others in order to fit in.
They will seek to satisfy other people,
to the point of losing any sense of what would satisfy themselves.
Piece by piece, they will lose themselves and their dreams.

Giving up on your own joy is a form of living death.
It brings a sorrow that, left unchecked,
will become your way of being,
like a numbness robbing you of the ability to feel.
Do not allow this to be your truth.

Rally yourself into action and seek a passionate, fulfilling life.
Choose to thrive instead of just to survive.
Look inside and find what makes you excited.
Breathe life into that part of yourself.

Who you are and what you enjoy matter.
Your Soul sings when you live with passion.
Quit searching for the meaning of life,
and decide to give it meaning on your own terms.
This is your birthright in Spirit.

173

EMBRACE YOUR INTUITION

Each Soul comes into a physical body
in order to experience what it needs to grow
and more fully understand itself and its connection to existence.
The Soul has a blueprint of circumstances, opportunities,
and challenges that are needed for its evolution.
Your intuition helps to inform you of what is coming up on your path;
it also serves as a spiritual compass-correction
when you stray from the road
your higher Self has chosen for you.
When you align with your intuition,
you step into a state of Grace.

The deep urges and subtle pulls that you feel
will be your intuition guiding you to where you need to be.
These urges serve to increase your awareness and comprehension of aspects of your life.
By learning to connect with your sense of inner knowing,
and by choosing to act on what you receive through
Intuition, you are embracing your Soul-Self.

Your Soul knows why you are here and what is best and needed most for you.
Live your life with a deep knowing that you are led
and that everything in your life has meaning and purpose to your Soul,
even that which is unpleasant.

Know that everyone has intuition and that it is up to you
to develop a connection with,
and an understanding of, this amazing inner voice.
Allow your thoughts, choices, and actions
to be led from the highest, most sacred part of you.
In this way, you are certain to walk a blessed path
of knowledge and understanding.

174

STAND STRONG IN WHO YOU ARE

Do not let outside forces change you.
The only changes that have value arise from within.
It is important to define your character and your way of relating to the World around you.
To gain happiness, you must know yourself and what matters to you.
You must allow yourself to live and express that truth in order to thrive.

Far too often, individuals lose themselves in a moment.
They will allow themselves to morph
into whatever they think will be accepted or will lead to the least conflict.
Often, these ideas of acceptance and conflict exist only within their minds.
They will project their own limiting thoughts onto those around them.

Aside from self-created limitations,
you will be faced with those who do not align with your way of being.
Accept this without the need to change them or yourself.
In this moment of acceptance on your part,
you become free to determine if this is a person
you want in your life or not,
without falling into condemnation because of differences.

Change, grow, and evolve.
This is the nature of your being.
However, let that growth be along your own path.
Seek to know your higher Self and allow all changes
within you to stem from that awareness.
Accept differences and do not sacrifice yourself for,
or ask for sacrifice from, other people.
To know yourself and to stand proudly
in your identity is a great blessing.
It is the integrity necessary
to experience a truly joyful life.

175

CAST ASIDE COMPARISONS

You cannot ever hope to have achievement
if you cannot envision yourself as the achiever.
You must first see yourself as successful
before you can experience true success in your outer World.
Many people believe they are incapable,
especially when they compare themselves to others.
They will assume that other people are surely smarter,
more capable, or somehow more equipped to succeed.
Often, they will fool themselves into believing
that things will somehow be easier for others than for themselves.
They may even allow themselves to think that Spirit itself is holding them back.

Some will hold these limiting mindsets
to the point of paralyzing themselves into inaction.
Some will simply give up, falling into a state of existing instead of living.
Their dreams, desires, and happiness will all be set aside,
because they cannot see themselves
as capable of having them realized.
Many will never even try.

To live this way is a denial of truth.
Cast aside comparisons.
Let go of competition.
The only contest you are in is with yourself,
and the only way to win is through self-acceptance and self-reliance.
Spirit does not choose to bless some and withhold from others.
You are born from the creative force of the Universe.
You are a part of everything that is.
Knowing this, how can you be limited?
Begin to see yourself in this magnificence.
You may doubt yourself,
but you should never doubt Spirit.

176
TURN INWARD

All of Creation resides within you,
and you within it.
Take comfort in this.
Remember that you are a Soul first
and that everything in your life radiates from your Soul-Self.
Many individuals become so focused on external challenges
that they will forget this one great truth.
However, the truth is that the Universe
is giving them what they truly need to grow
instead of simply satisfying wants.

The Soul desires growth and connection.
It knows only love and truth.
It craves the experiences that lead the lower self back
to the understanding that it is connected to the Divine.
The negativities you experience are meant to turn you back to your faith.
The positive ones are to remind you of the joys found in Spirit.

Turn inward and begin to focus on seeking personal growth.
See everything in your life as signposts leading you back
to the understanding that you are a Divine being
and that everything in this life is fleeting.
It is not meant to last, but rather to show you the way back home.
Have faith that all is as it should be.

Go within and ask what you need to learn from your present circumstances
and you will find the freedom to change them.
Live from within and with the complete understanding
that what you experience outwardly in this life
is but a reflection of what you are
at your innermost Self.

177
INVEST IN YOUR INDIVIDUALITY

Diversity is the essence of Spirit.
It manifests itself in a myriad of different ways,
each as much a part of the wholeness of the Divine as any other.
Therefore, to judge people by their individuality is to judge Spirit.
Many relationships, from the casual to the romantic, suffer or fall apart
because some people want others to mirror them in every way.
They want the people they connect with to think
and respond to the World in the same way they do.
They leave no room for difference in appearance, beliefs, or actions.

Sadly, some will sell out their truth for the sake of being accepted.
This acceptance, however, is hollow, as it is based on false appearances
and constructed out of fear.
To find those who accept and validate you just as you are is an amazing gift.
To find those who celebrate your individuality is priceless.

Invest in your individuality.
What makes you unique is what makes you special.
Celebrate the diversity that is all around you.
Decide today that you will spend more time
on finding points of connection with others
than you do focusing on differences.
Many of these differences, when combined,
create an energy of possibilities
that were not there individually.

Spirit is diversity made manifest.
The creative force of the Universe
will continually find new ways to express itself.
By seeing this as an absolute truth,
you will open yourself to a greater connection
to all that is.

178

LET THE PAST BE PAST

Once something reaches
its natural ending point, allow it to rest.
Avoid the urges to reexamine what once was.
Many thankless hours are wasted by dwelling on what has passed.
Some people will become so stuck in the past
that they are robbed of the present moment.
They allow their past choices and actions
to be their present identity,
even when they have grown and changed.

Choose not to define yourself by the past.
When you are confronted with a challenge, seek resolution.
Go within yourself and choose the response you wish to offer to the situation.
Live your highest truth and offer your most honest response.
Then, regardless of outcome, let go of the moment.

Rest comfortably in the knowledge that you did
what you could and responded the best you are able.
Learn what you can and allow that understanding
to empower you in your future endeavors—
but do not allow passing moments to become lasting identities.
Who, and how, you once were
need have no power over how you choose to be in the present.
Make bettering yourself
and your responses to the World around you
your strongest focus.

Realize that the past in no way defines you,
and decide who you are going to be in the now.
This is the liberation of free will
and the power of living in the present.

179

THRIVE IN YOUR IDENTITY

If you could see yourself as we do,
you would never again question your greatness.
If you were able to clear away the self-deprecation,
comparisons, and judgment and see yourself through your own Soul,
you would realize just how beautiful you are, how perfectly blessed and magnificent.

It is only the small view of the lower self that leads to suffering.
You are your own worst critic, sometimes believing that you
have failed or fallen short of serving purpose and
of having a meaningful life.
To live at all is to have meaning.
Your identity is your purpose in this life.
Even your presumed failures are merely moments of experience
to be added to the collective whole of your Spirit's journey.

Believe in yourself and know that your Soul-Self knows only joy.
It accepts everything that exists as a part of a great Oneness
and sees your part of that as no less wondrous
than the mightiest mountain or the stars above.
Everything in Creation is tied to, and a part of, everything else.
The true magnificence of Spirit lies in its wholeness.
Each piece shines with the light of the Divine and has significance.

You have purpose.
You matter.

Invest in the knowledge that you are who you were meant to be
and are in the perfect circumstance to find your true joy.
No matter what is happening in your life, you are fulfilling your Soul's purpose.
You are living the life your higher Self has chosen.
Choose to grow joyfully.
Thrive in your identity.

180

DON'T MAKE EXCUSES

It's crucial to realize when your connections
have shifted from comfort to dysfunctional familiarity.
Be diligent in discerning what used to serve your greatest good, but no longer does.
And be bold in finding the clarity and strength to let go of what was,
so that you can fully grasp what could be.

Many people cling to outdated and limiting identities
and circumstances in their lives.
They cling to these, because they are familiar and,
often, these conform to others' expectations.
People cling to the troubles that they know,
out of fear that change could lead to worse.
This is a dangerous mindset
that can only lead to unhappiness and self-limitation.

Cast off the chains of the limiting familiar
and understand that you are not obligated to negativity.
Strive to understand the difference between comfort and excuses.

Let faith carry you through the transition from who you were
to who you are meant to be in the now.
Grant yourself this freedom and allow your willingness
to change to be the cornerstone of your joy.
Then build upon that joy one experience at a time,
always moving forward, until you have
constructed a life of happiness
that reflects the truth of your inner self.

Only you have the power and authority
in your life to create lasting joy.
Let that awareness lift you up
to new perspectives and possibilities.

181

SHINE YOUR LIGHT IN THE WORLD

Just as the Sun shines its light on the World
each new day, so should you let yours shine.
Each of you holds a beautiful light of Creation
that shines from deep within your Soul.
That light can uplift, inspire, and lead others to their own greatness.
It can illuminate dark times, uncover hidden truths,
and ignite beauty within others.

Even when the clouds cover the Sun,
you still know it shines behind them.
Choose to be this way yourself.

The hardships and challenges of life
will try to diminish your light; shine anyway.
Others will attempt to rain on your joy
because of their own pettiness; shine anyway.
At times, you will not even believe in your own Self.
You will think that hope is lost
and sadness is your only choice.
It is not.

Especially in these moments,
shine as brightly as you can.
Optimism and faith go hand in hand.
They are the fuel that keeps your light
burning brightly.

182

BE AN EXAMPLE TO OTHERS

The difficult times in your life serve many purposes.
They help you grow and understand yourself more fully.
The experiences you gain
empower you to greater responses in the future.
They also give you opportunities
to exemplify faith and light to others.

Instead of allowing your hardships to become your identity,
choose to make them moments when your light shines the brightest.

Be an example to others.
Just as a match lights when pressed against a hard surface,
so you ignite into light and warmth when struck by life's challenges.
Set aside your need for others to know your problems.
Decide to let them see your solutions instead.

Shine brightly with faith and belief that you can rise above
and persevere through anything.
Find your inner fire and fuel it with self-love,
healthy relationships, and an awareness of your connection to the Divine.
Then your Soul will become incandescent,
shining like a beacon of hope for others to see.

Knowing you have the power to illuminate and uplift,
why would you ever choose darkness and sorrow?

183

BE STRONG

Allow yourself to see yourself as powerful.
Yes, physical strength is a great thing.
It reflects health and a deep caring for the Self
and grants you the ability to cope
with demands of the physical World.
Yet, it is not only physical strength that matters:
strength of conviction is essential.

In this life, you will often be known by what you stand for.
To have conviction is to care deeply and to act with integrity
according to your highest held beliefs,
regardless of the approval
or acceptance of others.

Decide also to be strong in your words—
not in their delivery, so much as in their meaning.
You do not have to speak forcefully for your words to be powerful.
They need only be truthful and spoken without fear or hesitation.

It is also necessary in this life to have strong boundaries.
Your ability to set aside your burdens and help others is another great strength.
Being selfless when another is in need
enriches the life of the giver and receiver both.
You can also find strength in your faith.
Grow in your connection to the Divine
and you will become stronger than you can ever imagine,
able to respond to life's challenges with grace and ease.

Every point of strength is amplified in its power
when it comes from a place of love.

1814
CHOOSE TO LOVE

To be strong, begin by loving yourself fully and without condition.
Establish this self-love so fully that it cannot be shaken or distorted by others.
Then, share that love with the World.

Love heals.
It uplifts the downtrodden and empowers the doubtful.
Love has the power to transform people and situations
and is the greatest reflection of your Soul's true nature.

Many will talk about love making them weak.
They will speak of poor choices and actions all in the name of love.
This is not love.

Real and honest love is returned to those
who offer it and is not reserved only for romance.
It empowers everyone involved.

Choose today to be strong.
Choose to love.
Develop a sense of power
and ability in all areas of your life,
but remember always to let this strength stem from your heart space.
Let love be the guiding force in your life and you will become
stronger than you ever knew.

185

BE THE CHANGE

Don't be the one who waits, the one who refuses to go first,
the one who won't say, "I'm sorry," because the other person should, too.
Don't be the one who wants to make a connection but doesn't out of insecurity, or
the one who wishes he had said, "Hello," "I miss you," or "I am sorry."
Don't give in to the fear that others won't like you,
that you aren't good enough, that you don't matter.

Don't limit yourself.
Don't allow anyone else to, either.
Quit being hurt as a way of gaining attention.
Let go of who said what and of the need for that to matter.
Quit allowing your happiness to hinge on someone else's actions.

What happens in your life is sometimes within your control, and sometimes not.
How you respond to what happens fully and without question is within your control.
You can run from the lessons involved,
only to find yourself facing them in new circumstances in your future—
or you can embrace the moment your Soul has led you to,
with the full knowledge that you are
capable of great things.

Find freedom through taking action.
Humble yourself enough to learn from what is happening around you.
Balance experience with your highest ideals and then act accordingly.
Be the one who is known for doing.

Be the first.
Be the one.
Be the change.

186
LET YOUR ACTIONS SPEAK FOR YOU

Let your actions be your voice in this World.
Be known for what you have done more than what you have said.
Many people make the mistake of talking about their plans
and aspirations far more than they actually pursue them.
They will speak of grand ideas and desires,
but never follow through with the necessary actions.
Some will even push this to the point where they are known by this trait.
This tendency to speak boldly and act meekly is a dangerous way to live.
Over time, it becomes a comfortable pattern
that leads to a true lack of ambition and sadness.

You were meant to live your life, to fulfill your dreams,
and to thrive in the boundless possibilities of your experience.
Let your actions define you so strongly that your identity is clear to all who see.
Set your intentions, but realize that it is actions
rather than intentions that make things happen.
Be a positive force of change in your own life
and the lives of those you touch.

Decide that today is the day to quit talking and start doing.
In the moment this occurs, you will have stepped into real control of your destiny.
There is a great comfort that comes from knowing you have done all you can,
a satisfaction that comes from personal effort.
This is the cornerstone of true happiness
and a key to self-mastery.

187

STRIVE FOR PEACE IN YOUR INTERACTIONS

To live in a state of inner calmness is a great blessing.
Peace and calmness should stem from a deep sense of love
and compassion for all people you encounter.
Always interact with the awareness that the other person
is just as much a part of the Divine as you are.
There will be times, however,
when confrontation becomes necessary.

When presented with argument or challenge
be strong within yourself and your responses,
but do not confuse strength with aggression.
Maintain inner peacefulness even in these moments.
Refuse to allow others to determine your demeanor.
What they say is up to them.
How you allow it to affect you is up to you.
Learn to speak your truth calmly and directly.
Be big enough to admit fault when you are in the wrong,
but do not allow others to berate you.
Remember always that people are more important than situations.
Choose to honor those with differing opinions by remaining gentle with your words.
Learn to walk away from those who would make differences a point of attack.
Let go of the need to convince unreasonable people.
Avoid those who would make being argumentative
their way of approaching life.

Embrace a peaceful nature,
even if that requires you to be the calm within a storm.
Do not sacrifice yourself, nor demand that of others.
Remember always that your Soul craves peace
and that you are indeed capable of strength
and calmness all at once.

188

LIVE WITH GRATITUDE

Gratitude has the power to transform your life.
By adopting a thankful attitude,
you place your focus on what is good and right in your experience.
This focus adds energy to your expression and causes good things to multiply:
such blessings will spread to other areas of your life.

What is not as easily accepted
is the goodness of holding gratitude for your challenges and burdens.
In such instances, it is not about being thankful for, or focusing on, what is wrong.
It is about being thankful for the gift that is always hidden
within a difficult situation: the opportunity for personal growth.
The wise person accepts that everything that happens in life
contributes to growth and understanding
of one's true nature.

When faced with challenges
choose to be thankful for the opportunity to grow,
have gratitude for your own perseverance,
and appreciate your ability to respond through choice instead of reaction.

Celebrate what is good in your life,
and do not limit this to merely what is pleasant and preferable to you.
Broaden your understanding of what good means.
The beauty of a rose is not lessened by its thorns, unless that is the only part you focus on.
In the same way, many situations in life are valuable,
even though certain aspects are not preferable.

Choose to live with gratitude,
and your life will give you more and more reasons
to continue being thankful.

189

GO WITH THE FLOW OF LIFE

You are ultimately in control of the direction life is headed.
You alone have the power to create or destroy happiness in your World.
This happiness is most easily found when you align with your higher Self
and allow your life to flow easily from that awareness.
Your Soul has set you on the path that is right for you
to experience everything you need to grow and be joyful.

Think of your life as a boat on a river.
Your higher Self is the flow and current of the water.
As you navigate through this river of life, you will have many choices
and opportunities to direct and control what is happening.
You can paddle strongly or just let the current carry you.
You can move quickly or slowly, depending upon your actions.
You have the choice to enjoy the view or simply withdraw into yourself.
You can, at times, find a new branch of the river and change course entirely.
You can stop along the bank at any point.
You can even take moments to play in the water.

All of this is an incredible amount of control over where your life is headed,
and yet you are still being carried by the current created by the higher Self.
Can you see why paddling upstream is pointless—and fruitless?
Why would you work so hard to fight
against the direction your Soul has chosen for you?

Trust yourself and go with the flow of your own life.
Let the current created by your Spirit
carry you to a place of wondrous growth and incredible happiness.
Accept where you are in your journey and trust that it will lead to where you need to be.
While you are indeed the Captain of your own ship, the voyage of your life will be
more satisfying when you allow the highest part of your Self
to be the navigator.

190

EXPLORE YOUR INNER TRUTH

Seek to understand yourself and your inner motivations.
Ask yourself often why you do the things you do,
say the things you say, and make the choices that you make.
Moreover, ask if these expressions are actually yours
or if they come from outer examples and expectations.
Refuse to allow yourself to live your life focused solely on the surface actions,
never delving into your motivations.

Many people try to change their outer actions and fail.
This is because they have not also shifted their inner motivations.
When you are motivated out of anything other than your Soul's truth,
you are bound to sorrow and emptiness.
However, when you shift your motivation away from the expectations of other people and align
it with your inner truth, you will find satisfaction and fulfillment in all areas of your life.

Choose to embrace the path of self-understanding and mastery.
It is the path to happiness.

Allow your responses to life to come from
a place of deep understanding of your own self.
Decide that what others think of you is theirs to deal with
and that it need not have any effect on you.

Strive to uncover your truth.
Let that understanding be your motivation in all things,
and you will rise to greater personal heights
than you ever imagined before.

191
SPEAK IN THE LIGHT

Be the one who chooses not to complain or fall into gossip.
Stand in your integrity and don't give into petty ways of speaking.

In this World it becomes a challenge for all
to not be drawn into complaint or small minded comments.
Everywhere you turn, people are allowing negative exchanges
to pass for social pleasantries.

Complaint and gossip share certain qualities:
neither is a full representation of the truth, and both are steeped in negativity.
They both serve as distraction from what is good and right with the World.
They are sad moments that are lost to the need to be small and petty.
What benefit is there to wearing your burdens as a badge of honor?

What is the motivation for such negative words?
Those on the Spiritual Path understand that
such ways of communicating do not reflect the nature of the Soul.
Embrace empowerment for the Self by speaking about
the good in your life rather than what is wrong.
Show compassion for other people
by being the one to walk away from conversations
about them in their absence.
Talk to people, not about them.

Learn to treat others as you would prefer they treat you.
Honor yourself and everyone with whom you interact
by focusing on positive and energizing exchanges.
Be the one who has the strength to say that
you do not want to join in with negative talk.
Offer other topics when confronted with such behavior.
If you truly wish to walk in the light,
begin by speaking within it.

192
ACCEPT WHAT YOU CANNOT CONTROL

Strive to understand the difference between what you can
and cannot control in your World.
Many people become frustrated with their lives
because they cannot control certain aspects.
You will face unbidden hardships.
You will age.
And, in the end of this part of your Soul's journey,
your physical body will die.

Many things will be beyond your control,
especially in your interactions with others.
Some of the most frustrated and angry people suffer
because they feel they can control everything in their reality.
They will ignore the fact that their lives are shared experiences
happening in a place full of other individuals with free will,
none of whom are obligated to behave
as they would demand of them.

Some will choose anger as their response when they feel their control slipping away.
Others will try to exert their control, regardless of proof
that they have no authority in the situation.
They will use shame, guilt, and manipulation
to try and coerce others into their way of thinking and acting.
Some people become so controlling
that you would believe they could tell the Sun not to rise.

By learning to accept what you cannot change,
you free your focus and direct energies
toward things you are able to affect.

Your attitudes, responses, and happiness are all choices for you to make and act on.
It truly is your responsibility to create the life you desire.
You have incredible power over who you are and how you approach your life.
This is the awareness that leads to a feeling of control and satisfaction.

193
CONTROL YOURSELF

If you wish to change others, do so by example.
Weed your inner garden rather than focusing on the weeds
others allow to grow in theirs.

Begin within.
Learn to control your thoughts and emotions.
Let go of the need for others to act according to your demands.
Exert dominion over your own self and your outer experience will shift to match
what you have established as your way of inner being.

Let this self-control radiate out and change your circumstances.
Indeed, take direct actions to change things that are not right in the World,
but do so with discernment, choosing not to waste time and energy
on things you will surely have no effect on.
Be the change you wish to see,
rather than pointing out where others are not.

By learning to understand what you can and cannot control,
you will have both freed and empowered yourself
to be a force of change and goodness in the World.

You will have enabled yourself
to live in happiness.

1994

STAND TALL

Stand tall and confident in your identity.
Even though you may not match other people in opinion,
physicality, or status, be proud of who you are.
Let your convictions and highest thoughts
define you to the point where there is no room for question.

Accept the circumstances of your birth and upbringing.
They are part of who you are.
You have given your entire life to be where you are right now.
Do not undervalue that.
Work tirelessly in the areas of self-growth,
but allow all goals and aspirations to be of your own choosing.

There will always be those whom you see as blessed
in some way you wish were your own,
and those whose experience looks more painful than yours.
Rest assured that you do not know their entire story, nor they yours.
Comparison can lead only to jealousy or vanity.

Be fearless, accepting yourself so fully
that the opinions others hold about you do not matter.
You came to this place, this life, to express your truth,
not simply to imitate and regurgitate the truths of others.
Realize your potential and then live up to it.

195
TAKE OWNERSHIP OF YOUR LIFE

Personal accountability
is a cornerstone of Spiritual growth.
Let go of the need to blame other people
for your present circumstances and attitudes.
Take responsibility for where and who you are in life.

Whether you act through weakness or empowerment is your choice alone.
Happiness and sadness are as well.

Your attitudes and responses should evolve as you grow
in your understanding of your own self.
Simply put, you should respond differently as an adult than you did as a child.
Your responses come from your free will.
To blame another person for your actions
is to give away your power and freedom of choice.
All people have bad things happen to them in life; that is not their fault.
However, once they understand the cycle of cause and effect,
their actions are indeed their own fault.

Let go of your hurts rather than allowing them
to harden you and limit your possibilities.
Blaming others is easy.
However, it is fleeting satisfaction
compared to self-empowerment and ownership of your life.
When you truly let go of blame and claim authority in your attitudes and actions,
then you also claim your right to happiness.

Be your own person and savor
the joy that comes with this choice.

196
EMBRACE YOUR FREEDOM AND RESPONSIBILITY

Your life is not happening to you.
It is responding to you.
You are an energetic being,
vibrating at your own unique frequency.
You are a force of Creation made manifest in the World.
Your attitudes, choices, and actions are energies
that radiate from you into the Universe.
The Universe reflects those energies back to you
in the form of experiences and situations.
This, in turn, gives you new opportunities to learn and grow,
refining what you choose to send into Creation.

In this way you are the teacher, student, and the lesson in your own World.
You are the cause and effect, the problem and the solution.

Once you understand the cycle of attitude
leading to expectation, of expectation leading to creation,
of creation leading to experience, and of experience leading back to attitude,
you begin to understand the driving force behind all of your life's situations.

You, yourself, create all of your circumstances.
This is both an incredible freedom and a great responsibility.
Everything you experience, every situation happens
as a result of your innermost expectations.
Your experiences manifest from deep within your expectations
and beliefs about yourself.

Therefore, the key to a happy life is a happy attitude.
Should you want success you must first see yourself as successful.
Walk, talk, and act as you want to be.

197

ASK FOR ANSWERS AND TRUST THE PROCESS

It's okay not to know the answer.
There will be times in your life
when you're uncertain as to which actions are best.
It is normal in these times to feel fearful and apprehensive,
especially when change is imminent but unclear.
Not knowing what comes next challenges confidence, conviction, and even faith.
Uncertainty in one area of life can cause you to doubt yourself in other areas as well.

Many will judge themselves harshly for being uncertain, while others will take random actions,
hoping to make something happen so they can move from the place of unknowing.
This reckless approach often creates more problems than it solves.

When you are unclear as to the best course of action, begin by finding calmness.
This alone will bring clarity to your mind that may allow an answer to emerge.
Beyond this, humble yourself enough to ask for help.
Often, those around you can see your situation with greater clarity than you can for yourself.
This does not mean you should simply do what others want.
It means that, when you allow it, the answers you seek will be everywhere you look.

Trust yourself enough to recognize the truth when it is presented to you.
Remember also the power of patience.
Sometimes the best action is to do nothing in the moment.
Often the crisis will pass and the right choices
will become evident with just a little time.
Beyond all this, remember who and what you are.

Your Soul does have the answers you seek.
That part of you led you to this place.
Trust and know that the answers you seek
will become evident when
the time is right.

198

BE SINCERE IN YOUR INTERACTIONS

Do not fake who you are and how you express yourself.
Be genuine and real, regardless of how you may differ from others.
Let go of the need to impress.

There is no person, place, or thing
that is worth losing the truth of your identity for.
Establish a sense of personal integrity
that you take into every situation and connection in your life.
Strive for absolute honesty, both inwardly and outwardly.
Understanding who you are and what your personal truth is,
and then living it boldly and without apology,
is the very essence of empowerment.
Be proud of who you are, not because of circumstances of your birth,
but rather because of your choices and actions in life.

Make your identity so strongly rooted
and established in your higher thinking that you are a living example
of Spirit made manifest in this World and carry your head held high because of this.

Many people lack sincerity and will even resort to lies
and deceptions in an attempt to portray themselves in a way
they think will be accepted by others.
Others will create an identity they feel gives them control and power.
You already have great power, and it comes from being sincere and living truthfully.

When you live from a point of personal truth an incredible thing happens.
The Universe will respond by sending people
and experiences into your life to validate you.

Strip away the masks and false words.
Fly free in your true identity and you will soar
to greater heights than ever before.

199

DON'T SWEAT THE SMALL STUFF

Learn to let small things be small things.
Move away from the need to exaggerate what is going on in your life.
Do not allow minor obstacles or distractions
to become excuses that keep you from your chosen path.
Life is full of twists and turns and there will be times when you have to respond.
However, it is far too common a practice
simply to drop motivation over the smallest of excuses.
There is no reward for lack of effort.

The only true limitations are within your mind.
Everything else can be worked through, gone around, resolved,
or even ignored for the sake of forward movement.
Let go of the need to focus on how difficult your goals are
and begin to celebrate each and every step toward attainment.
Let this feeling of success and accomplishment
hold far greater space in your mind
than all of the reasons why it is hard.

Become relentless in your pursuit
of personal goals and excellence.
See yourself as capable and you will be.
Your goals are yours to attain.
You are equipped for greatness and success.

Become an unstoppable force
for positive changes in your life.
Make things happen.
You are greater
than your challenges.

200

TAKE THE HIGH ROAD

In order to be truly happy,
you must become a source of happiness for others.
By choosing to embody happiness itself and share that feeling with others,
you will infuse it deeply into your consciousness
and make it a natural part of your expression.
Many people deny themselves
the joy that comes from lifting someone else out of despair or sadness.
Your situations do not determine your attitude.
You do.

When you give circumstances power over how you feel, then you are owned by them.
Situations will become the driving force behind your moods
and interactions with others.
This need not be so.

Empower yourself to rise above any situation.
Set aside your problems as often as possible
and devote your efforts toward helping others,
even if that is just a kind word or gesture.

When you allow yourself to uplift others
you are embracing and embodying the energies of resolution and freedom,
and you are then able to direct those same energies toward your own circumstances.
Being in service to others is a blessing to them,
but an even greater one to your own self.
When you find yourself at the crossroads of hurtful and helpful,
remember to take the high road.
It will lead you to great joy,
while the other will only lead you to a dead-end path
of sorrow and loneliness.

Choose to be helpful
and you have already chosen
to be happy.

201
BE THE BEST PERSON YOU KNOW HOW TO BE

Loneliness and self-doubt
often push people into connections
that are hurtful and damaging.
There are a great many people living in negativity
that revel in the chance to criticize someone else
rather than address their own shortcomings.
You are a bright shining Soul expressing itself in a unique and individual form,
and you belong here as much as anyone or anything else in Creation.
Your outer World reflects your inner thoughts and feelings.
Therefore, if you wish to find love and acceptance outwardly,
you must begin inwardly.

Cherish your individuality and sacrifice it for no one.
Find the strength, the faith, to embrace yourself fully and to walk in your truth.
When you do this with confidence and certainty,
you will see the energies of love and acceptance returned to you.
Be true to yourself and realize that you owe no one else an explanation about this truth.
You are accountable only to your own self.

Set that standard and expectation high, and live up to it constantly.
This is the way of the empowered individual:

Be the best person you know how to be.
Set an example in every choice and action you take
and allow yourself to validate your own efforts.
You are magnificent,
regardless of the shortsightedness of those who cannot see it.
Believe this with all your heart
and the Universe will find amazing ways
to validate that magnificence.

2021

BE THE HERO OF YOUR OWN STORY

Decide today
that you do not need anyone else to rescue you,
fix you, or change your life for you.
Be empowered with the understanding that
all challenges you face are within your ability to resolve.
Many people spend their lives in a fairy-tale mentality,
believing that there is someone on a white horse
who is meant to save the day for them.
They allow negative circumstances to continue
without attempting to right the situation on their own,
out of a belief that someone else will do it for them.

The danger of expecting someone else to rescue you
is that it breeds a victim mentality
that causes the helplessness to worsen.
Many people will use their hardships as a means of manipulating others
into doing things for them.
Some will see assistance as the affection they are missing
in other areas of their life
and will adopt helplessness as a way to feel loved.

Stand tall in your ability to manage your own life.
Act heroically toward yourself.
Do for yourself what you wish someone else would do for you.
Realize that you are far more capable than you have believed before.
Know that you need no saving because you have decided to rescue yourself.
Act boldly when faced with challenges.

Be bigger than your problems,
stronger than your adversities,
and own your personal sense of power.
When you do this your World will shift
from a place of challenges
to a place of opportunities.

203

IF YOU WANT TO BE BLESSED, OWN YOUR DIVINITY

To be blessed
you need only accept that you are a part of Creation
and equally as important as everything else in existence.
This may seem difficult to accept and validate,
and yet it is the truth that all of the great prophets
and mystics have spoken.
It is one truth that is and ever shall be.

Many deny themselves blessings
because they feel they do not deserve them.
They will hold themselves lacking because of self-judgment
while blaming the Universe for their circumstances.
Some believe that their blessings come from humbling themselves
and identifying themselves with their suffering.
While you should hold gratitude for your existence
and be thankful for each good thing in your life,
you should also realize your Soul's light and allow that grand illumination
to lift you to a state of elevated experience.
When you are faced with turmoil and troubles,
acknowledge that you are blessed to handle such burdens.
When you struggle, find blessing in perseverance.
Beyond all else, be blessed by your faith.

Invest in a firm belief that all is as it should be
and that whatever befalls you will lead you to a greater truth,
a more pure expression of your Soul's identity.
If you want to be blessed, own your Divinity
and acknowledge yourself as a mighty Soul,
connected to all that is.

You were born blessed.
You need only remember the truth
of what you are and all will be open to you.
It is a choice and it is yours to make.

2044

LOVE YOUR SHADOW-SELF

The path to the highest Self is often a journey
through the lowest aspects of your identity.
It is normal to think of this as a perilous path,
to want to distance yourself from the parts of yourself
that you do not like.
The desire to be more than one presently is can become
a self-protection born of self-loathing and harsh inner judgements.
Often, people will exaggerate their better attributes to draw attention away
from what they wish others will not notice about them.
All of this effort would be better served
in making real changes,
but some feel inadequate to the tasks.

The truth is that you cannot change anything about yourself
without first connecting to it: it is your present truth.
When you accept and own your shortcomings,
you have stepped into a space of empowerment
and enabled yourself to make real and lasting changes.

Embrace your limitations and make them a focus in your desire to grow.
Be at one with your whole self and step into your personal challenges.
Only then can you instigate transformation.

Walk this road with confidence.
Own your shortcomings.
When you deeply connect with them and listen to them
as the loving parent listens to the child, you will find the ability to change.

Bring your shadow-self out of hiding
and into the light of self-awareness and acceptance,
and you will have already begun a magnificent transformation of yourself
and your experience in life.

205

TAKE BACK YOUR POWER IN NEGATIVE CIRCUMSTANCES

You will find many things upsetting and frustrating
as you journey through this World.
At times it will be situations that anger you;
at others, it will be people.
While anger is unavoidable, losing your temper is not.
To give in to your anger is a choice to allow negativity to control you.
In the moment you lose your temper, you have given up self-control.
The people and situations you face in this moment
will dictate your words and actions, and you will be lost unto yourself.

Regardless of what you are confronted with,
you have free will to choose your responses.
What someone else does is their karma.
What you choose as your response is yours.

Loss of self-control resolves nothing,
but retaining your power of choice and self-expression
will lead you to contentment regardless of what you are facing.

Take back your power in negative circumstances.
Choose the way you wish to carry yourself, and refuse to waiver from this expression.
Even when action is required, remain true to your highest Self.
Set boundaries, speak out about wrongs, remove negative people from your life,
and be a force for positive changes where these are needed.
Do all of this while remaining centered and calm.

Decide today to change situations
rather than allowing them to change you.
In this way you can take something negative
and make it a moment for growth
and positive action.

206

BECOME THE LIGHT-BEARER FOR YOUR OWN JOURNEY

Your body is the temple of your own Soul.
Your Spirit does not dwell within the buildings or the teachings of others.
The expansiveness of your Soul cannot be revealed by books or dogmas.
Though many people will tell you they have the one absolute truth, this cannot be so.
The Sacred Path is an individual journey
that leads to understanding of the Self and, ultimately,
to the realization that everything in this life is temporary:
you do not belong in this place
but are merely passing through it to learn and grow
on your Soul's journey home.

You cannot find your truth solely by external means.
Only by looking within can you discover your true Spirit
and its expression and understand the totality of your being.

Care for this body and make it strong and healthy.
What you do to your physical self you ultimately do to your Soul.
Within this awareness, allow your choices to become simple.
Be led by the knowledge that you carry a sacred light
and that good actions will allow that light to grow.

You are not a body that happens to have a Soul.
You are a Soul that has chosen a physical form
for the sake of experiencing this World to learn and grow.
Empower yourself with these understandings and decide
to let your inner light shine into all corners of your existence.
Choose to illuminate your own reality: show your true self to this World.
Become the Light-Bearer for your own journey
and follow that light into truth and happiness.
The power is yours.

207

BE AT ONE WITH YOUR OWN STRENGTH

Everyone faces self-doubt and fear.
Insecurity is a natural state of being,
so do not harshly judge yourself when confronted by it.
It is quite normal, especially when striving to move forward,
that you will struggle against it.
The former self will grasp and cling desperately
to hold you within old patterns of existence.

Growth will depend upon letting go
of what was for the sake of what could be.
In this letting go, it is natural to feel the loss of the old self and to mourn.
Do not let your mourning overvalue the past
when a brighter future lies before you.
Honor who you have been by building upon
that experience and rising above it.

Place your focus and efforts on the future Self.
It is in the now that you can affect what will be.
Acknowledge your fears, understanding
that courage is not the absence of fear
but the willingness to move forward in spite of it.

Be at one with your own strength,
and commit to overcoming self-doubt and fear.
The moment you realize your own magnificence,
the entire Universe will reverberate with a newfound energy,
and the World will open up to you.

208

BEGIN TODAY

There is no time like the present.
No matter your age, your background, or your self-imposed limitations,
you have the power to begin anew right here, right now.

Break out of the bonds of limiting thoughts.
It does not matter where you come from or where you have been.
It matters where you are going and
who you believe you will be when you get there.

Your social status, how much money you have,
or any other perceived limitation is meaningless.
Great and amazing things have been done by people of all ages and all walks of life.
It is the belief that what you want is possible and that you deserve it,
coupled with real efforts toward your goals,
that will bring your joys to fruition.

Begin today.
Set your goals and decide what you can do here and now to move toward them.
Reject limiting thoughts from others, but even more so, from yourself.
Empower yourself with expectations of greatness
and put effort, every single day, into what you desire.
You deserve to be happy, but only you have the power to make it so.
The time is now.

209

TRAIN YOURSELF TO BE AMAZING AND MAGNIFICENT

Just as athletes must train daily to win at their game,
so must you train your mind daily to win at the game of life.
By deciding who and how you want to be
and embracing the diligence necessary to master your own thoughts,
you create a very defined energy of creation that will go before you.
This energy will create opportunities for you to act upon
that will begin to shape your outer World
to match these inner thoughts.

In truth, you are creating your own experience right now.
Most do so unconsciously, allowing their previous
experiences or childhood programming
to determine what thoughts they are sending into creation.
You must begin to root out these deep-seated thoughts.
You have to decide which thoughts need to be removed
and what they will be replaced with.

Learn to meditate, making it a daily practice.
Take time each day to set your intentions, review, and change the inner dialogue,
to establish new and positive thinking as your normal way of being.
These new thoughts are best supported by following through with
self-validation of the changes you are making.

Be grateful for the awareness of what needs to change.
Likewise, be thankful and celebrate each moment you succeed
in replacing an old habit with a new action.
Change yourself and the World around you will change as well.
Believe in the power you hold over yourself
and free yourself to take charge of your experiences in this life.
Train yourself to be amazing and magnificent.

210

OPEN YOURSELF TO NEW EXPERIENCES

Be willing to change your approach to life
when your present actions are not fulfilling your needs.
By breaking out of familiar patterns and habits,
your can shift your entire experience in life.
Everyone faces fear and insecurity
when it comes to breaking out
of the familiar into the new.

Do not let familiarity become a burden.
Do not let comfort become a limitation.

Push yourself toward new behaviors that more closely match
what you want in life and feel good for each step you take.
Be bold in your new expressions,
but realize that there will be need for adjustments as you go.
Give yourself time and patience as you explore your new self.
Avoid self-criticism as you settle into new patterns.

Do not be reckless in these new pursuits,
but do embrace diligence and a commitment
to rise out of the self-created ruts of your life.
This is a wondrous acknowledgement of your Soul's limitless capacity.
You came to this World to discover your true Self.
Become the explorer of your own Soul's truth.
Be willing to change and try new ways of expressing yourself.
Only then can you discover your personal truth
and the joy that comes from living it.

211

FIND LOVE WITHIN

Love is one of the most powerful forces in the Universe.
It has the ability to uplift, to heal, to validate, and to empower.
This is especially true when it is directed at the self.
Many people suffer from wanting to feel love
from someone else when it is impossible,
for they have not learned to love themselves.

They will spend time and effort on appearances,
hoping this will bring someone to love them.
This may lead to attraction or sexual interest, but it is not love.

Unfortunately, some cannot tell real love from kind words or attention.
They think so little of themselves that they will fall in love
with anyone who speaks or acts kindly to them.
Their desperation to find love will cause them to settle
for whatever attention they can get.
They will cling to the idea that love conquers all
and suffer greatly when it does not.

Learn what love actually is and feels like by loving yourself fully
and then hold all others to this same criterion.
Love is acceptance.

Begin within, establishing a loving relationship
between your physical self and your Soul.
Be as invested in yourself as you wish someone else would be.
Love yourself just as you are.

When you do this, you will open yourself
to a new energy that will draw in others
who love you, as well.

212

BE THE EMBODIMENT OF GROWTH AND CHANGE

Do not waste your time
trying to fix people who would rather remain broken.
As sad as it may be, some people want to be in shambles.
They cling to their burdens as their identity
and no matter what efforts you put into helping them,
they refuse to grow and change.
At best, they ignore what would change their situation.
At worst, they will expect someone else to fix things for them
while holding no personal responsibility.

Decide today not to live your life in this way.
Realize you are capable of a much greater personal expression.
To be in service to others is a grand and noble thing.
Helping those in need is the mark of one who is on the Spiritual Path.

However, you must choose to place your efforts wisely.
Be certain before intervening that your assistance is wanted
and not born out of your self-driven need to control.
Seeing another's potential is wonderful when it inspires her or him to strive for greatness,
but pointless when that individual refuses to move toward it.
At times your very heart will ache when struggling and suffering
while refusing to change things.
In these times you must practice acceptance.

By finding the balance between allowing people to live their own truths
and helping when it will actually do good,
you are honoring your own desire to uplift others while respecting their free will.
Be the embodiment of personal growth and change.
When you live in this way, you will find yourself in the right energy
to help those who wish
to grow and change.

213

CELEBRATE EACH SMALL ACCOMPLISHMENT

By celebrating
each small accomplishment along the way,
you create an energy that will carry you to your goals.
Goals are important, but they are meaningless
without validation and follow-through.
Many people have lofty ideas
about what they wish to do with themselves or their lives,
but they believe that their challenges are too great to overcome.
Their focus on negativity will magnetize like-minded people into their World.
They will find themselves surrounded by individuals
who have also abandoned hope and settle into a lower way of being.

This is dangerous company to keep.
They will try to hold you in a space of self-limitation
that frees them from having to do anything about their own issues.

Likewise, when you choose to find within your own Self
the motivation toward your goals and validate those efforts,
your energy will attract amazing new people into your life.

By forming this relationship first with the Self,
and secondly with a group of strong supporters,
you are empowering yourself for great accomplishment.
You are capable of overcoming your challenges.
It can be no other way.

Let your inner dialogue become one of self-praise instead of self-criticism.
Let your outer voice match this and you will find yourself
surrounded by loving individuals who share in your joy.
When you choose to validate yourself,
the entire Universe will respond.

2114

BE HERE, NOW

Being fully in the present is what matters most.
It is in the here and now that you live.
In this exact moment only do you have the freedom
and choice over your expression and experiences in life.
Who you may one day be is constantly shifting
because of your choices and actions in the now.
The past need not, and the future simply cannot, define who you are.
Only your expression in the present holds your identity.

Some will judge their past actions so negatively
that they don't feel they deserve happiness at all.
Likewise, many people will miss the joy that is in front of them
because their thoughts are so deeply invested in the future.
Sadly, many of one's imaginings about the future have no basis in reality—
they are fears or dreams that will never come into being.

Who you are presently erases who you once were
and aligns you with who you will be.
Therefore, bring your focus to the present.
Remember and learn from the past.
Plan and work toward the future that you desire,
but do these while remaining in the present.
In this very moment you are free to be yourself,
to express the truth of your Soul's identity.

215

COMMIT TO YOURSELF

Many people wrestle with commitment.
This can be seen in their relationships, goals, and ideals.
Often you will see people wavering back and forth over their choices.
They will seem unable to devote themselves fully to one course of action,
always looking for something better.

Many people will make excuses rather than to commit to anything at all.
They fear they are giving up their free will and the chance to act,
should something better come along later.
Sadly, this often keeps them from delving deeply enough
to find the true value of their situations.
They have failed to commit to themselves and,
because of this, they do not trust their own judgments.
When you commit to yourself, you take responsibility for your choices and actions.

Self-commitment helps establish your core beliefs, values, and self-worth.
Self-commitment helps you know yourself so well that your decisions become easy.
This level of discernment makes all of your choices obvious.
It grants you the luxury of knowing to whom and
what you want commit yourself in life.

Commit to yourself and, using that self-devotion as your base,
establish strong commitments to the people, situations,
and aspirations that fit comfortably with your Soul.
When something complements your inner Self,
commit to it fearlessly.

216

SEE THE COLORS IN THE TAPESTRY

Learning to see
things from other people's perspectives is a skill that will serve you well in life.
Understand that not everyone sees the World in the same way that you do.
All people come into this life to express their Souls' truth.
That, along with their life experiences,
will dictate how they see each circumstance as it comes along.
They will respond to situations from their own understanding, not yours.
By setting aside the urge to call anything other than what you would do as wrong and striving
to understand the motivations and choices of others,
you have blessed them yourself with a broadening of your own mindset.
Learn to listen to others with the intent to gain understanding
rather than to correct them.

Avoid dealing in absolutes.
What may be truth for one person may not be truth for another.
Everyone's story holds some piece of understanding or insight for you.
Even if it is an awareness of how you do not want to live,
you will have gained something in the exchange.
It is important to remember that everyone is a part of Spirit
and that one expression is just as valid as any other.
This does not mean you should allow the truths of others to pull you from your own path.
It does not mean you should sacrifice what you know to be right for your own Self.
Aside from that which threatens you,
strive to live in acceptance of the differences of those around you.
When you accept people as they are rather than trying to change them,
you see the beauty in diversity.

It takes many different colors of threads to make a beautiful tapestry.
Begin to see people as the individual threads that weave together in Spirit,
and you will honor each Soul's expression
while inviting harmony with your own experience.

217

BE THE EMBODIMENT OF HAPPINESS

Make happiness an attitude—a way of approaching life—
rather than an emotion dependent upon certain outcomes.
Make joyfulness one of the focal points of your existence,
independent from what is going on around you.
You will feel every emotion possible as you move through the experiences
and circumstances of your life.

However, those on the path of awareness understand
that these shifting feelings are meant to be temporary;
they do not have to become your identity.
It is possible to be happy even in troubling times.
This becomes easier when you decide to choose your identity and expression
rather than letting life's circumstances dictate these for you.

For those who choose happiness as their identity,
the dark times in life are made lighter.
They understand that the moment of sadness or anger
will give way to their positive outlook and, because of this,
they will begin to impact the situation rather than letting it define them.

Of course you must feel all emotions.
Situations in life will come and go, each bringing an opportunity
to experience yet another aspect of your own Self.
Live in the moment.
Feel what you feel.

Be the embodiment of happiness.
Honor every experience
and learn all you can about yourself.
Make that part of you unchangeable
and a new experience will open up to you.

218

SEE YOUR REFLECTION IN THE WORLD

If you wish to understand your inner nature,
simply look at the World around you.
Everything in your experience is a reflection of your own energies.
The people and circumstances that are present in your life
mirror your own inner vibration:
they are there because on some level you invited,
allowed, or expected them to be there.
The events of your life are not random;
neither are the people with whom you find yourself interacting.
Everything is there to give you greater understanding of your Soul's truth
and to urge you along your journey.

For many this awareness will be troubling.
They will look at the difficult people in their lives and have a hard time accepting
that these individuals hold a gift of understanding and growth for them.
They will have trouble believing that the people they struggle with the most
represent the greatest opportunities to re-create the self.

Much wasted effort has been spent trying to change outer circumstances
when the only real change comes from within.
As you change your relationship with your own Self,
the circumstances of your life will shift as well.
Circumstances will change, relationships will fall away,
and new ones will be established.

Take time to go within, evaluate the people and things in your life,
and find higher definition for the Self through this awareness.
Your life is a mirror for your Soul, and you alone are in control over the reflection you see.
Shine brightly and the World will show you the beauty of that light
reflected back at you everywhere you look.

219

EMBRACE PASSION

To live without passion is merely existing, not thriving.
Seek within yourself to understand what makes you feel most alive
and align yourself with this as your identity:
this will lead you to experience true happiness.
Many people spend countless hours doing what they feel they must
rather than what brings them joy.
They will limit their lives to walk, talk, and act like those around them.
Most will let go of the very things that would give them great joy,
because these seem unimportant
when weighed against the demands
and expectations of the World.

How can happiness not be a priority?
Why is following your own inner guidance
and living your individual truth so often unsupported by others?
It is difficult for most people to validate another's passion
because they are unable to do the same for themselves.

You must be prepared to leave some behind when you decide to step forward.
While it should be obvious that you must take care of your responsibilities in life,
you must realize that you are also responsible for your own happiness.

Embrace passion.
Let it motivate and drive you.
Become the thing you love most and be joyous in its expression.
When you begin to understand that you either live with passion or with limitation,
the choices in your life become easy.

220
ALLOW THE FRUIT TO RIPEN

Divine timing is a blessing that can be,
at times, hard to acknowledge and accept.
People have their own agendas and their own sense
of when things should happen for them.
They will set their expectations deeply within their minds
as to when and how things should unfold.
Most often, theirs are self-imposed timeframes
and have nothing to do with the natural order of events.

The Universe seeks to fulfill your expectations.
It conspires within itself to enable you to achieve that which you desire.
However, where you are and where you want to be in life
can often be more distant than first thought.
The changes being sought may require more shifting than you realize.
Have patience and couple it with perseverance.
Do not easily let go of ambitions, especially because of timing.
Trust that by holding fast to your vision,
even when nothing seems to be happening,
you are still moving toward fulfillment.

Do what you are able in every moment,
even if that is just holding faith that things will work out.
Know that your Soul is timeless and allow that to calm your
anxiousness about your present circumstances.
Everything changes and you have the power
to affect those changes as they occur in your life,
but the wisest understand that these things
will happen in their own ways.

Embrace patience within Divine timing
and you'll be embracing the power
to be happy in the here and now.

221

CELEBRATE THE JOYS OF OTHERS

Do not begrudge the good fortunes of others,
even when you face adversity in your life.
Jealousy tears apart relationships and leaves the one
living in comparison feeling less as a person.
The jealous will often criticize those to whom they compare themselves,
seeking any way to detract from others' joy or blessings.
They will allow their own pettiness
to keep them from joining in celebration, congratulations,
or even interactions with those who are living the lives they want to have.
Even those you feel are better off than you have their own struggles.
Likewise, the seemingly lowest ones among you
carry the blessing that they are bright, shining Souls.

Spirit knows only equality.
All beings have purpose and significance
and all will experience highs and lows in their lives.
It must be this way for the Soul to grow and evolve.
When you see those who are experiencing something wonderful in their lives,
step away from jealousy and adopt the attitude that you too deserve greatness.
Allow them to be examples of self-worth and the power of inner expectation.
By joining in their happiness, you will shift your energies
to magnetize goodness into your own life.

Choose also to be a grand example
for those who are struggling.
Learn to celebrate the joys of others
and to uplift the downtrodden whenever possible.
The ability to see beyond your own personal experience
is a magnificent blessing and expression
of your Soul's truth.

222
CHOOSE THE DAWN

Make optimism your approach to life,
even when faced with adversity.
The energies you express will either amplify
or lessen what is right or wrong in your life.

Unfortunately, many insist on viewing the World
as a never-ending set of challenges.
Because they fail to see themselves as the solution, there will be none.
However, those on the Spiritual path understand that every crisis
is an opportunity and every challenge a chance to grow.
They will choose to remain happy and optimistic
regardless of their circumstances,
because they know that this choice will change
what is happening for the better.

Such people appear to live charmed lives when,
in truth, they simply have good attitudes.
They expect things to work out and will learn something of value in the process.
Because of their approach to life, they will attract situations,
remedies, and opportunities that uplift them
from their burdens and one good thing
after the next will happen to them.

If you seek to find what is wrong in this World,
you need not look far.
Likewise, should you seek good,
which is all around you in abundance.

In the darkest night of the Soul rests a choice.
You can curse the darkness
for keeping you from seeing how to move forward,
or you can have faith that the dawn will reveal new options
to you in its breaking light.

I'm a Shaman — It's What I Do
Postscript

"I don't think there's a hell and I'm not convinced that God is as mad at us as they have tried to tell us." I was all of ten years old when my mother told me that. Looking at her with the wisdom that we all know a ten-year-old possesses, I said, "Mom, I know." That's where it began. Though beyond my child's understanding at the time, my mother was about to embark on a life-long quest that would lead me—lead us both, actually—to where we are today. I had been brought up in a Baptist church and had recently felt "the calling." I still talk about it. There I was in church, singing. This in itself should have kept me from hearing anything Divine at that moment, but somehow Spirit got through. I felt the Spirit's calling and was saved. It was the most profound moment of my life. I felt for the first time a true connection and closeness to God. And I wanted more. I needed more. But that was all that church had to offer. Its mission had been fulfilled and, from that point on, it was up to me to attend and say the right words at the right time.

That simply wasn't going to cut it. So my mom, who felt the same yearning for more, began taking me with her to various other churches, groups, meetings, seminars and workshops. We tried everything from Assemblies of God to Zen Buddhism, with each step leading us further from "organized religion" and toward "metaphysics" and spirituality. I guess I shouldn't have been surprised. Looking back, I remember my mother telling me to go outside and play with "my friend." It was my Spirit Guide and, fortunately, my mother never told me that he was imaginary. We'd also talk to my grandmother. It never occurred to me that that wasn't "normal," though she had killed herself before I was ever born. We'd just sit in the living room and talk to her. It seemed quite uneventful at the time—and it still does, for that matter.

In time, we were led to The Hilltop Center, Betty's house. Betty opened her home to the public every Wednesday evening to teach metaphysics. It was a place to meet like-minded people in an open, supportive environment. I met psychics, channelers, astrologers, spiritualists, and healers there, learning something from each. I remember one man in particular named Hank. He shook my hand and told me that I was going to be famous for my voice and that I would be on the air, but not seen. He was right: four years later, while still in my teens, I began a ten-year career as a radio disc jockey. Hank also told me that I had a gift and that I would use it to help people one day. At the time, I thought he was just a funny old man. But others were saying much the same thing—like Barb, Spirit Woman. We met her at Hilltop; soon, we'd be visiting her at her home.

I was twelve years old when my mother first drove me to visit Barb. I remember our drive through the Ozarks countryside. We found her living in an old house in the Missouri woods. It felt both magical and very real, this house, this woman, these woods: each seemed rooted in the Ozarks and yet connected to some higher mystery. I know now that mystery and reality are one and the same, though, at the time, this was a lesson still to be learned.

We visited Barb for my mom's sake. She was going through some hard times in her relationship with my stepfather and decided to seek out the advice of this medicine woman who did readings. Did I know that this woman, that house, those woods would confirm my spiritual path and come to help me define myself and my life's work? Again, I was only twelve years old.

We walked in and sat at her kitchen table. Spirit Woman sat down with us and started talking to my mother about her situation. I had never witnessed anything like this before. She seemed to know everything about my mom. It felt spooky and fun, all at the same time. After a while she turned to me and said,

"I have something very important to tell you as well. You are a reincarnated Shaman and you are going to continue that work in this lifetime." Of course, I didn't understand what I had just been told. I didn't know what a Shaman was beyond what I had seen on TV and in the movies. Besides, I was ready to embark on adolescence and had other interests in mind, as you might imagine.

The more my mom and I visited her, the more insistent Barb became. I was a Neo-Shaman, she'd tell me, and I would help people in the same way Shamans had throughout time in virtually every culture, but I'd do it in a modern context. I remember just laughing. But as she talked, Spirit Woman described experiences that I had been having throughout my childhood. She knew me in a way no one else did, as if "from the inside." For example, she told me about my adventures in "flying." When I was very young, I'd sit on my bedroom floor and put my baby blanket around me as my cape. Soon, I'd be looking down on myself from the ceiling. It was just a game back then, but I know now that these out-of-body experiences were my first attempts at Shamanic Journeying.

Barb used to get migraines and would ask me to put my hands on her head to make the pain go away. I thought it was fun, since it got me so much attention. But, truth to tell, I was beginning to sense that my sense of "normal" was far from the "normal" of schoolmates and friends. I had long felt that I was "different" somehow from other children my age: we had the "real world" in common, but the mysteries connected to that "real world" seemed to elude them. So, when Spirit Woman offered to train me in the ways of the Shaman, "I went along for the ride," just as I had done with my mother in visiting her.

Very shortly into the training, I began to hear voices. Some people think "hearing voices" is a sign of madness, and I suppose it can be in some cases. Even people who are open to spirituality have trouble understanding this notion—and I don't blame them, since it's so hard to describe. It is, however, easy to experience. Consider it this way: it seems as if we think our thoughts, but words often pop into our heads freely and of their own accord. Everyone has experienced this, right? Christian tradition—and I was raised Southern Baptist, remember—talks of that "quiet voice" inside each one of us. Here's a more mundane example. Let's say you're driving and feel your eyesight pulled down to the dashboard and see the fuel gauge on empty. Do you think that's mere chance? Or, say, something inside you tells you to slow down and you're glad you do, because a child has just darted out onto the street to fetch a ball. "Watch out" or "Don't do that," you've said to yourself. Sometimes you've listened—and sometimes you've regretted that you didn't. But is it you, or one of your Spirit Guides, that's directing your attention or giving the words? Spirit-guidance is so naturally a part of our daily lives that we often can't distinguish our words from those of our Guides—until we practice spiritual listening and learn to do so. While we all have native intuition, a Shaman consciously develops this inward skill of listening and of talking back.

Soon, I learned to distinguish the different voices of my Spirit Guides. I gave myself over to the training, and the things Barb showed me seemed quite easy and natural. I developed my intuition and ability to direct energy, both for healing and for manifestation. Then the day came that she insisted that I start doing readings for people. I went out and bought a Tarot deck and started reading for people out of fun. I was fifteen and really didn't believe in myself as a reader as much as I trusted Barb and was following her lead. That feeling from being saved in the church returned. I came alive when I would talk to people over the Tarot cards. People's responses were enthusiastic and validating; they said the information that came through was accurate and helpful, and, for my part, as I noted before, I liked attention. I began to realize that Barb was right. Although I was the one getting the attention, I wasn't the one giving the messages. The messages weren't coming from me—they were coming through me. I was becoming a "conscious channeler" and Spirit was laying down some truths. I found myself talking to people about the most intimate and difficult aspects of their lives, often speaking about things I had never personally experienced or even thought about.

Once I had proved myself, Spirit Woman gifted me a naming bundle and called me "ShadowHawk, a Shaman of the people." That is when I made the promise to Spirit. I vowed to help those that I could with my abilities and formally committed myself to the Neo-Shamanic Pathway that I have walked ever since.

I returned to Hilltop, this time as one of the core psychics of the group. I also began to draw on the many different cultures that included Shamanic Practitioners. I was amazed at how one experience or teacher led to the next. I learned of Soul Retrieval and Journeying. I was taught to work with animal totems and spirits.

I began working with a hypnotherapist who took me further than I was able to go on my own. She helped me let go completely and become a freer channel. Using hypnosis, she would put me under and ask for the Guide to speak. She would get the name of the individual asking for guidance and relay it to me. I would then see a book of that person's life and start talking. At that point, all became a blur to me as the other consciousness spoke through me. The response was mind-blowing. I can say in complete humility that we truly helped some people.

Through all of this I have developed quite a relationship with my own personal Spirit Guides and have gotten quite comfortable in my Neo-Shamanic identity. Many people take that for arrogance. It is actually a profound sense of being one with the all. That connection empowers us in a way that nothing else can. It is our Spirit that sustains us and, through it, we are a part of all things. So often, clients come to me seeking their purpose in life. I feel very blessed to know and be living mine.

As with all aspects of life, our paths and priorities shift over time. We stopped doing readings together and each settled into our individual work. I devoted myself to working with people on an intuitive and energetic level and developed a long-standing practice as a Shaman and Intuitive Counselor—work I am still very much devoted to today.

I began teaching yoga as well and opened Sage Studio in Springfield, Missouri. The yoga seemed to fit perfectly with my other spiritual/energy work, and having an actual "workplace" outside of the home proved a nice change. I got so busy that I brought on an assistant, Jann. One day, after I had spent a week sick in bed, Jann messaged me with an idea: "I think you need to write something inspirational every day. You know, let 'them' talk through you and just put it out there for everyone." Considering this was the first day I could even hold my head up after being so sick, I wasn't much interested in any new project. She wouldn't let it go. After several texts back and forth, I agreed and told her I'd try it the next morning. I got up that day half expecting frustration. I didn't feel particularly inspirational at all, but sat down to meditate to gather my thoughts anyway. I found myself slipping into an old familiar feeling. That presence, my Guide that I work with every day, was there in a different way again. I remember in my mind saying, "What? What do you want to say?" The next thing I knew, my fingers were flying on my keyboard as I watched the first Spirit Message of the Day appearing on the screen in front of me. This happened for the next 222 days in a row. Each morning I would sit and ask what was to be said; and as I slipped into semi-consciousness, the words would begin to appear. With each day, the process became easier and easier. And the messages, which I originally posted on Facebook, really seemed to help people, which has always been my biggest aspiration.

What Spirit Woman told that twelve-year-old proved true. Throughout my life, I have been blessed by the presence of my Spirit Guides and am so truly thankful that they have worked through me to help others. It is my hope that the words in this book help you as well.

All these years later I am still learning, still trying to grow spiritually. In my Neo-Shamanic practice, I offer readings in person, by phone, recorded on cd, or by email. I travel throughout the Midwest doing workshops and "reading days" in people's homes. I teach people about their Spirit Guides and Animal Totems and do healings whenever called for. It is challenging and rewarding work. I'm a Shaman ... it's what I do.

The Spirit speaks through number sequences as well as words, and there's good reason why my Spirit Messages continued for 222 days. In her website, "Angel Numbers" (http://sacredscribesangelnumbers.blogspot.com/), Joanne Walmsley makes several observations:

> Number 222 is made up of the attributes of and energies of number 2 appearing tripled, making number 222 a very powerful vibration. Number 222 carries the attributes of the numbers 2 and 22, the Master Builder Number

that resonates with ancient wisdom, vision, idealism and transformation. Number 2 lends its influences of faith and trust, encouragement, attainment and success, adaptability, diplomacy and co-operation, duality, service and duty, balance and harmony, selflessness, faith and trust and your Divine life purpose and soul mission. Number 222 has to do with balance, manifesting miracles and new auspicious and timely opportunities.

Angel Number 222 encourages you to take a balanced, harmonious and peaceful stance in all areas of your life. The message is to keep the faith and stand strong in your personal truths.

Angel Number 222 tells you that everything will turn out for the best in the long-term. Do not put your energies into negativity— be aware that all is being working out by spirit for the highest good of all involved.

Angel Number 222 is also reminding you to keep up the good work you are doing, as the evidence of your manifestations are coming to fruition.

Angel Number 222 is a message of faith and trust from your angels. Remember that nothing happens by chance and everything happens for a reason. Maintain a positive attitude and you will find that everything will have positive results and you will receive abundant blessings in Divine right timing.

She's right. There's a carefully interwoven tapestry in the 222 Spirit Messages presented here: faith, trust, self-respect, internal balance and harmony, a positive attitude—these are all building blocks of happiness. But, much like musical notes, these need to be composed and arranged and performed on a daily basis, with all the variations that daily life affords. If there's something in these Spirit Messages "for everyone," then there's surely something in them for you, personally.

—Shane Knox, a.k.a. ShadowHawk

Index of Messages

1	Live Fully in the Moment
2	Let Experiences Nourish the Soul
3	Reclaim Your True Nature
4	Remain True to Your Higher Beliefs
5	Value—and Validate—Your Own Needs
6	Listen to Your Inner Voice
7	Be One With Nature
8	Rise Above It All
9	Claim Your Place
10	Celebrate Your Uniqueness
11	Seek Within
12	Fly Free
13	Celebrate Your Body
14	Own Your Truth
15	Visit Your Temple
16	Accept Your Life
17	Remember Your True Purpose
18	Welcome the Kind Words of Others
19	Find Compassion for All
20	Focus on Yourself
21	Create Your Truth
22	Stand Strong
23	Focus on the Spiritual
24	Choose Your Company Wisely

25	Step Into the Dance
26	Forgive For Your Own Sake
27	Own Your Mistakes
28	Live Fully in the Moment
29	Know You Are Not Alone
30	Don't Give Up
31	See the World as Your Mirror
32	Let Go of the Old to Embrace the New
33	Bless Others
34	Know Yourself
35	Decide Now
36	Create Your World
37	Decide That You Matter
38	Be What You Want to Experience
39	Let Go of Guilt and Worry
40	Live in Faith
41	Take Time to Play
42	Remember Compassion
43	Create Your Intentions
44	Honor Your Oneness With Spirit
45	Know You Are Watched Over
46	Be Slow to Judge and Quick to Validate
47	There's No Need to Explain
48	Be Yourself
49	Make Love a Way of Life
50	Keep Your Composure
51	Show and Tell Your Love
52	Find Your True Family
53	Act, Don't React
54	Accept Yourself
55	Speak Your Feelings
56	Give Up Regret
57	Learn to Let Go

58	Meet Criticism With Honesty
59	Create Your Inner Peace
60	Choose Optimism
61	Connect With Spirit
62	Own the Self
63	Speak Your Truth
64	Let Your Light Shine
65	Live Spiritually
66	Be Open to Change
67	Be Quick to Forgive
68	Create the Life You Choose
69	Life Is Not a Competition
70	Don't Judge the Present by the Past
71	Make Gratitude Your Attitude
72	Bring Joy to Life
73	Stick to the Plan
74	Live Free of Regrets
75	Accept and Respect
76	Give Up Gossip
77	Feel Fully—and Then Let Go
78	Learn to Laugh at Yourself
79	Be Bold With Your Ambitions
80	Embrace Your Uniqueness
81	Learn Patience
82	Lead by Example
83	Have Faith in Dark Times
84	Avoid Other People's Dramatics
85	Revel in Kind Words
86	Create Positive Energy
87	Build a Positive Self-Image
88	Don't Expect Others to Change
89	Let Go of Comparisons
90	Be Inspired by Creation

91	Show Gratitude
92	Choose Your Reality
93	Speak Out Against Wrongs
94	Listen to Your Inner Voice
95	Look for Beauty
96	Make a Difference
97	Seek Self-Mastery
98	Wed Emotions to Reason
99	Accept What Is
100	Value Effort Over Outcome
101	Help Yourself by Helping Others
102	Speak Your Truth
103	Slow Your Pace
104	Let Go of the Past
105	Take Time for Silence
106	Choose to Believe
107	Re-Create Yourself
108	Be Yourself, Not Your Situations
109	Learn to Let Go
110	Create the World You Want by the Words You Speak
111	Take Pride in Your Body
112	Learn From Your Mistakes
113	Exercise Your Power of Choice
114	Quit Making Excuses
115	Empower Yourself
116	Embrace Those Who Embrace You
117	Do Not Run From Your Challenges
118	Learn to Give and Receive
119	Avoid Complacency
120	See Your Soul-Self Reflected in Others
121	Know That You Are Worthy
122	Stand in Your Own Truth
123	Do What Is Right

124	Become One with What You Seek
125	Accept People as They Are
126	Honor All Paths
127	Embrace Compassion
128	Forgive Others, Forgive Yourself
129	Be a Force for Change
130	Strip Away All Falsehoods
131	Find Enlightenment in Letting Go
132	Let Go of Worry
133	Act as You Speak, Speak as You Think
134	Embrace Change
135	Practice Gratitude
136	Affirm Other People's Choices
137	Ask What You Are Here to Learn
138	Be Bold in Living Your Truth
139	Avoid Jealousy
140	Be Active in Your Spirituality
141	Value Yourself
142	Choose Happiness
143	Treat Others as You Would Be Treated
144	Heal Yourself by Helping Others
145	Let Your Actions Speak for You
146	Let Faith Sustain You
147	Don't Give Up
148	Love Yourself in Soul and Body
149	Celebrate Others' Differences
150	Create Your Own Identity
151	Challenge Yourself
152	Seek Empowerment
153	Relax and Let Go
154	Speak As If in Prayer
155	Speak Through Love
156	Be Self-Centered, Not Selfish

157	Remember Your Soul-Self
158	Be Generous
159	Love Yourself Unconditionally
160	Give Love Freely and Without Expectation
161	Feel the Presence of Lost Loved Ones
162	See Loss as Change
163	Avoid Complacency
164	Choose Your Path
165	Honor Each Person's Choices
166	Let Go of Self-Criticism
167	Choose Happiness
168	Find Happiness Within
169	Strive for Simplicity
170	Recognize Your True Value
171	Tend Your Inner Garden
172	Pursue Your Passions
173	Embrace Your Intuition
174	Stand Strong in Who You Are
175	Cast Aside Comparisons
176	Turn Inward
177	Invest in Your Individuality
178	Let the Past Be Past
179	Thrive in Your Identity
180	Don't Make Excuses
181	Shine Your Light in the World
182	Be an Example to Others
183	Be Strong
184	Choose to Love
185	Be the Change
186	Let Your Actions Speak for You
187	Strive for Peace in Your Interactions
188	Live With Gratitude
189	Go With the Flow of Life

190	Explore Your Inner Truth
191	Speak In the Light
192	Accept What You Cannot Control
193	Control Yourself
194	Stand Tall
195	Take Ownership of Your Life
196	Embrace Your Freedom and Responsibility
197	Ask For Answers and Trust the Process
198	Be Sincere in Your Interactions
199	Don't Sweat the Small Stuff
200	Take the High Road
201	Be the Best Person You Know How to Be
202	Be the Hero of Your Own Story
203	If You Want to Be Blessed, Own Your Divinity
204	Love Your Shadow-Self
205	Take Back Your Power in Negative Circumstances
206	Become the Light-Bearer for Your Own Journey
207	Be at One With Your Own Strength
208	Begin Today
209	Train Yourself to Be Amazing and Magnificent
210	Open Yourself to New Experiences
211	Find Love Within
212	Be the Embodiment of Growth and Change
213	Celebrate Each Small Accomplishment
214	Be Here, Now
215	Commit to Yourself
216	See the Colors in the Tapestry
217	Be the Embodiment of Happiness
218	See Your Reflection in the World
219	Embrace Passion
220	Allow the Fruit to Ripen
221	Celebrate the Joys of Others
222	Choose the Dawn

www.ingramcontent.com/pod-product-compliance
Lightning Source LLC
Chambersburg PA
CBHW051801100526
44592CB00016B/2518